W9-AAU-942

ADRIAN ROGERS

DISCOVER JESUS

THE AUTHOR AND FINISHER
OF OUR FAITH

innovo
PUBLISHING
innovopublishing.com

Published by Innovo Publishing, LLC
www.innovopublishing.com
1-888-546-2111

Providing Full-Service Publishing Services for Christian Authors, Artists
& Ministries: Hardbacks, Paperbacks, eBooks, Audiobooks, Music,
Screenplays, & Courses

Discover Jesus
The Author and Finisher of Our Faith

Copyright © 2020 Love Worth Finding Ministries. All rights reserved.

No part of this publication may be reproduced, stored in a retrieval
system, or transmitted in any form or by any means electronic, mechanical,
photocopying, recording, or otherwise, without the prior written
permission of Love Worth Finding Ministries.

Scripture taken from the New King James Version®. Copyright © 1982 by
Thomas Nelson. Used by permission. All rights reserved.

Some Scripture quoted is from the King James Version of the Bible and
noted with (KJV).

ISBN: 978-1-61314-574-6

Cover Design: Collin Houseal
Interior Layout: Innovo Publishing, LLC
Printed in the United States of America
U.S. Printing History
First Edition: 2020

CONTENTS

Introduction 5

Who is Jesus?

Who Is Jesus? 7

How to Know Jesus

How to Enjoy the Presence of God 21
Three Strikes and You're Out 33
No Other Way to Heaven Except through Jesus 47
What Shall I Do With Jesus? 61

How to Grow in Jesus

How to Be a Growing Christian 75
You Can Be Sure 89
Bible Baptism.. 103
How to Have a Meaningful Quiet Time..................... 113
How to Make Your Bible Come Alive 125
The Principles of Prayer 137

How to Share Jesus

Learning to Share Jesus 149
The Soul Winner's Six Mighty Motivations................ 161
Birthmarks of the Believer 175
How to Arrive at Our Destination Without a Map ... 183

INTRODUCTION

Looking unto Jesus, the author and finisher of our faith, who for the joy that was set before Him endured the cross, despising the shame, and has sat down at the right hand of the throne of God. (Hebrews 12:2)

D iscoveries are being made almost daily in our world. New medicines. New technologies. New stars and planets. New ways to do things with more efficiency and precision. New truths and new ideas. Our society loves to discover new things.

To discover is to find, to gain knowledge of, to notice, or to realize. We don't just like to discover new things, but we also like to find new facets of old things. It's a joy to find a lost earring or a lost twenty-dollar bill. In addition, there is something wonderful about recovering an old friendship or noticing something in the Bible that we never noticed before.

This book is all about discovering the Lord Jesus Christ. Perhaps, you met Him as a young child. Your life has been spent getting to know Him more and more. It could be that you found Jesus as a teenager or young adult. You've also enjoying gaining more knowledge of Him through the years. A few of you may have met Jesus later in life. For you, each day is a new adventure with Him.

It may be that you are picking up this book because you are curious about Jesus. You have heard about Him, but you may not know Him personally. Our prayer is that your journey through these pages will lead you to find and meet the Jesus you will read about. He loves you and wants to have a real and personal relationship with you.

For all of you who will read these chapters, we pray that God will give you such a renewed love for the Lord Jesus. May your time in this book and in His Word compel you to know Him and to love Him more. Truly, may you discover Jesus, the Author and Finisher of our faith.

WHO IS JESUS?

COLOSSIANS 1:12-21

"What's the world coming to? It's coming to Jesus."
—Adrian Rogers

S ome time ago, I watched a program hosted by Peter Jennings called, "The Search for Jesus."[1] As a matter of fact, I watched for a while and then could not watch any longer. So, I turned the television off and walked out of the room.

Honestly, I would just as soon watch a group of men with bags over their heads in a cave with a jar full of lightning bugs try to find the noonday sun as watch these people talk about their search for Jesus. Nothing definitive was ever discovered on the show because they were looking in the wrong place. Jesus is there to be found if you want to find the authentic, real, genuine Son of God.

Several years back, Bryant Gumbel was interviewing Larry King on CNN. Gumbel asked Larry King this question: "If you could ask God only one question, Larry, what would it be?" Larry King said, "I would ask Him if He has a Son."[2] Very interesting. Great question. And the answer: Yes. God does have a Son. And His name is Jesus.

Christian apologist John Blanchard has estimated that of all of the people who have ever lived since the dawn of civilization—

there have been about 60 billion people—only a handful have made any real, lasting impression and actually changed the world.[3] In addition, of that handful of people, there is only One who stands head and shoulders above all of the others, and His name is Jesus.

Also, more attention has been given to Jesus than to any other person in history. More devotion has been given to Him. More criticism has been given to Him. More adoration has been given to Him. More opposition has been given to Him. Every recorded word that He said has been sifted, analyzed, scrutinized, and debated more than all of the historians, philosophers, and scientists put together.

Yet, He lived over 2,000 years ago. And after 2,000 years, there is never one minute on this earth that millions are not studying what Jesus said. Think about it. Here's a person who lived in a tiny land two millennia ago, and yet His birth divides the centuries: BC and AD. "Before Christ" and "Anno Domini," are the years of our Lord.

Jesus never wrote a book and yet library after library could be filled with volumes about Him. Even more, multiplied millions of books have been written about the Lord Jesus. Although He never painted a picture, as we look around creation, we see His handiwork everywhere. Uniquely, the world's greatest art, drama, music, and literature has Jesus of Nazareth at its source.

As far as we know, Jesus never raised an army, yet multiplied millions have died for Him. He never traveled far from His birthplace, and yet His testimony has gone around the world. Jesus only had a handful of followers that were with Him in ministry, and yet over 30 percent of the world's population are Christians today. In fact, the largest religious group on earth follows Jesus.[4] Think about it...a public ministry of only three short years, and yet here we are, 2,000 years later, praising His wonderful name.

Likewise, Jesus had no formal education. He didn't attend a university or seminary, and yet thousands of universities and seminaries have been built in the name of Jesus Christ of Nazareth. In my humble, but correct, opinion, no one can call himself or herself educated who does not seek after Jesus Christ.

Historian Kenneth Scott LaTourette said, "Jesus has had more effect on the history of mankind than any other of its race who ever existed."[5] To explain Jesus Christ is impossible. To ignore Jesus Christ is disastrous. To reject Him is fatal. To know Him is to love Him. To love Him is to trust Him. To trust Him is to be radically, dramatically, and eternally changed.

Additionally, human speech is too limited to describe Him. In like manner, the human mind too small to comprehend Him, and the human heart can never really, completely, or totally absorb who Jesus Christ really is.

In Colossians 1:12, we read, "giving thanks to the Father who has qualified us to be partakers of the inheritance of the saints in the light." In this verse, we are talking about our inheritance. If somebody wealthy left you or me a legacy, wouldn't we be interested? Then pay attention to the next phrase: "He has delivered us from the power of darkness and conveyed *us* into the kingdom of the Son of His love..." (Colossians 1:13).

The entire text reads like this:

> ...in whom we have redemption through His blood, the forgiveness of sins. He is the image of the invisible God, the firstborn over all creation. For by Him all things were created that are in heaven and that are on earth, visible and invisible, whether thrones or dominions or principalities or powers. All things were created through Him and for Him. And He is before all things, and in Him all things consist. And He is the head of the body, the church, who is the beginning, the firstborn from the dead, that in all things He may have the preeminence. For it pleased the Father that in Him all the fullness should dwell, and by Him to reconcile all things to Himself, by Him, whether things on earth or things in heaven, having made peace through the blood of His cross. (Colossians 1:15-20)

Jesus doesn't just want a place in your life. He doesn't wish for prominence in your life. Ultimately, He deserves and demands pre-eminence. The scripture says, "that in all things He may have the preeminence." As you read today, consider three powerful reasons that Jesus deserves and demands preeminence in our lives.

JESUS REVEALS THE FATHER

In Colossians 1:15, we discover that Jesus is the image of the invisible God. God is Spirit: invisible, unfathomable, unapproachable. How can we know God? Through Jesus, who is the image of the invisible God. The visible Jesus makes the invisible God known.

How are you going to know God? Not by reason. How are you going to know God? Not by religion. How are you going to know God? Not by ritual. You are only going to know God by revelation. Indeed, Jesus Christ has come to reveal God to you. You can never fully know God the Father apart from God the Son.

In Colossians 1:15, we read, "He is the image of the invisible God, the firstborn over all creation." Consider those two words, *image* and *first-born*. The word *image* is the Greek word *icon*. Likely you have a cell phone, and you have icons on your phone. An *icon* is a representation. In the same token, Jesus is the *icon* of God. The Greek word for *image* means "the exact representation." Jesus is the express image of the invisible God. He is the icon of God.

If you read Colossians 2:9, you will discover how Paul sums it up, "For in Him dwells all the fullness of the Godhead bodily." All of God was in Bethlehem's babe. He is the icon, the express image of God. Do you want to know God? Jesus Christ has cornered the market. He has a monopoly on revealing the Father. This is the only way you're going to know God, and it is through His Son, Jesus Christ.

Matthew 11:27 shares what Jesus Christ Himself said, "All things have been delivered to Me by My Father, and no one knows the Son except the Father. Nor does anyone know the Father except the Son, and *the one* to whom the Son wills to reveal *Him*."

Either that's true or it's not true. I believe it's true. Jesus says, "Nobody knows My Father but Myself, and you can't know Him unless I introduce Him to you." That's a big statement. Why? Because Jesus is the express image of God. You're never going to figure God out. How can the finite understand the infinite? Not by reason, but by revelation. Any other god that you worship is the god of your guesses, and that's a form of idolatry. You don't conjure up some god in order to worship him.

This may sound narrow-minded. But we don't want to be so broad-minded our minds get thin in the middle. Nor do we want to be so open-minded our brains may fall out. For example, I want my doctor to be narrow-minded. I don't want him to say, "Well, you're sick. Here are ten bottles of medicine. Let's just take one of them and see what happens." Additionally, I want my airplane pilot to be narrow-minded and not try to land with the landing gear still up. Also, I want my banker to be narrow-minded and carefully account for my dollars.

So, why would I not want my theology and my eternal destiny to be narrow-minded? Truly, you can't know the Father apart from Jesus Christ. Jesus didn't say, "I'm A way;" He said, "I am THE way." He didn't say, "I am A life." He said, "I am THE life. I am the way, the truth, and the life." You see, God was manifest in the flesh.

My pastor friend Jerry Vines imagines Jesus Christ going into the temple and having a conversation with the teachers when he was a 12-year-old boy. As one of the learned doctors in the temple strokes his beard and says, "Son, how old are You?" "Well," He says, "on My mother's side, I'm 12 years old, but on My Father's side, I'm older than My mother and as old as My Father."[6]

You see, Jesus was both God and man. On His mother's side, He got thirsty; on His Father's side, He said, "I am the water of life." On His mother's side, He got hungry; on His Father's side, He took a little lad's lunch and fed 5,000. On His mother's side, He was homeless and didn't have a place to lay His head; but on His Father's side, He owned the cattle on a thousand hills. On His mother's side, He wept at the grave of Lazarus; on His Father's side, He said, "Lazarus, come forth," and raised him from the dead. He was God in human flesh.

Look at the word: *firstborn*, in Colossians 1:15. Don't get the idea that *firstborn* implies a beginning. Indeed, Jesus never had a beginning. In fact, He has always existed in a state, never a start. He didn't have His beginning at Bethlehem. There never was a time when Jesus did not exist. Regarding this, Jesus said in the Gospel of John, "Before Abraham was, I Am." He did not say, "I was." He said, "I Am." Jesus is the great I Am.

What does the word *firstborn* mean? The Jehovah's Witnesses tell us that there was a time when Jesus did not exist, that He was created.[7] Colossians 1:15 is one of the verses that they try to use for this argument. However, they mishandle the word *firstborn* altogether.

The word *firstborn* speaks of honor and privilege, as God said of David in Psalm 89:27, "Also I will make him *My* firstborn, the highest of the kings of the earth." "And He," Jesus, "is before all things..." (Colossians 1:17). He could not be created. Why? Because all things were created by Him. It is obvious that whether there are things in Heaven or things on Earth, everything was made by Jesus and for Jesus.

Would you like to know God the Father? Would you like to know what our great God is like? Who He is? Would you like to know His heart? Friend, Jesus reveals the Father.

JESUS RULES THE FUTURE

Not only does Jesus reveal the Father, He is also the image of the invisible God, the firstborn, the highest of all creation, and above all creation. Furthermore, Jesus rules the future; He rules the world and all of creation.

Look at Colossians 1:16-20 again:

> He is the image of the invisible God, the firstborn over all creation. For by Him all things were created that are in heaven and that are on earth, visible and invisible, whether thrones or dominions or principalities or powers. All things were created through Him and for Him. And He is before all things, and in Him all things consist. And He is the head of the body, the church, who is the beginning, the firstborn from the dead, that in all things He may have the preeminence. For it pleased the Father that in Him all the fullness should dwell, and by Him to reconcile all things to Himself, by Him, whether things on earth or things in heaven, having made peace through the blood of His cross.

Now what is this talking about? This passage is speaking about One who rules the universe. Indeed, Jesus not only has this whole world in His hands, but He has the past, the present, and the future in His hands. People ask, "What is the world coming to?" Answer, "It's coming to Jesus." It is coming to Jesus. "All things were created by Him and for Him," and all will climax in the Lord Jesus Christ.

Consider a few additional points about this passage. First of all, Paul says that Jesus is the power of creation. In Colossians 1:16, we read, "For by Him were all things created." The little baby in Matthew 1 is the mighty God of Genesis 1. There was nothing made without Him. John tells us, "All things were made by Him."

Do you believe in evolution? Personally, I do not. Truly, I wouldn't believe in evolution even if I weren't a Christian. It's the next best guess of those who do not know the Word of God. If evolution is true, you will definitely have problems with the Scripture. If the Bible can't tell me from whence I have come, how can it tell me where I'm headed?

If you believe in evolution, you'll also struggle with matters of salvation. If there's no creation, no Adam and Eve, and no Garden of Eden, then there is no record about the fall of man and sin. Indeed, if there's no fall into sin, there's no need for a new birth.

Some people think man is just progressing onward and upward. But Jesus said in John 3, "You must be born again." If Genesis 3 is a myth, John 3 is a farce. If you believe in evolution, you're going to have problems in society, and that's why we have so many. As we've often said, if you teach the boys and girls they come from animals, it ought not to surprise us that they begin to act like animals.

Do you think all of creation just happened? Do you think it's just by some random chance? Did everything come out of some primordial ooze that came out of lifeless matter?

There's an interesting book about evolution called *Darwin's Black Box*. Scientist Michael Behe pried open Darwin's Black Box and mentioned a concept called *irreducible complexity*. In summary, this concept teaches you to reduce life back until you can't reduce it any smaller. And when you look at the simplest part, it is so complex that there's no way possible that just one cell could have come about by evolution. Truly, all of the components in that one cell are interdependent.[8]

In your own body, there are 10-50 trillion cells, all of them incredibly complex.[9] In just one cell in your body, you have rods known as *chromosomes*. And in these chromosomes, you have genes, or your genetic makeup. Your genetic makeup is determined by your DNA.[10] Scientists study DNA and say, "There's a mind there. There's intelligence there. There's design there. There's no randomness there."

Even more, in just one cell, there is enough information that it would take six hundred thousand books to write down the code of the DNA that is in one of the trillions of cells in your body.[11] DNA determines your intellect, the color of your hair, and your personality. Who did all of this? Jesus. "All things were made by Him." Jesus is the power of creation.

JESUS IS THE PRESERVER OF CREATION

In Colossians 1:17, we read, "And He is before all things, and in Him all things consist." Do you know what the word *consist* means? Things that consist stick together. Jesus Christ is the glue of the galaxies. What is it that keeps it all from falling apart or coming apart? Jesus.

In the same fashion, Jesus is the One who feeds the sun with its fuel. Jesus is the One who guides the planets in their orbit around the sun. Likewise, Jesus is the One who has set out all of the stars. Some people talk about natural law. There's no natural law. There are the laws of Jesus that nature obeys. It is by Jesus that all things consist.

Recently, I was looking at Isaiah 40:26: "Lift up your eyes on high, and see Who has created these *things*." Have you ever looked up at the stars at night or the sun in the day? That's what Isaiah tells us to do, "Lift up your eyes on high, and see Who has created these *things*."

Do you think that everything came out of nothing? You may say, "I can't believe in an eternal God." Do you believe in eternal, inanimate matter? Isaiah 40 tells us about God, "Who brings out their host by number; He calls them all by name, by the greatness of His might and the strength of *His* power; not one is missing."

One day, I was listening to the radio. During an advertisement, they suggested, "We'll name a star after you. You choose somebody, and we will name a star for that person, and we'll put it in a book." Too late. Every one of the billions and billions of stars already has a name. Jesus has named each one of them. He is the preserver of creation. He guides it all.

Did you know that light travels at 182,282 miles per second? How fast is that? Let's hijack a light beam and travel to the sun? The sun is 93 million miles away. You can be there in eight and a half minutes, traveling on a light beam. You want to go to the nearest star? It would take you four and a half years, traveling at 186,282 miles per second to get to the nearest star. That's 27 trillion miles away. And that's the closest one.[12]

In like manner, there are more than 100 billion stars in our galaxy. To go from side to side, rim to rim, in our galaxy would take you a 100 thousand light years, traveling at 186,282 miles per second.[13] Who did that? His name is Jesus. He's the One by whom all things consist. He is the power of creation. And, He is the preserver of creation.

JESUS IS THE PURPOSE OF CREATION

Look again at Colossians 1:16: "For by Him all things were created that are in heaven and that are on earth, visible and invisible, whether thrones or dominions or principalities or powers. All things were created through Him and for Him." Why was everything created? Do you think it is for you and me? No, it's for the Lord Jesus Christ. *For* is a preposition that speaks of direction. It's the Greek word "Τια." It means to be moving in the direction.[14]

Over the past few decades, we in America have been greatly influenced by Eastern religions. Eastern religions are circular, teaching that everything goes round and round. That's the reason they believe in reincarnation. I've always thought reincarnation was putting the milk back in the can. In Eastern religions, you have to live with good karma. And if your karma is not good, then in your next life you may come back as a roach. But if you've been good, you might come back as a cow. That's the reason they don't eat meat. You might be eating one of your relatives.[15]

However, the Bible teaches us that life is not all circular. The Bible is linear. We're moving to the time when the kingdoms of this world will become the kingdoms of our Lord and His Christ. That's the reason He taught us to pray in Matthew 6:10, "Your kingdom come. Your will be done on earth as *it is* in heaven."

Let me give you a verse my wife shared with me. It's Isaiah 33:22: "For the LORD is our Judge, the LORD is our Lawgiver, the LORD is our King; He will save us." Jesus is Judge, Lawgiver, and King. What are the three parts of our government? The judiciary (the judge), the legislative (the lawgiver). and the executive (the king). Did you know Jesus is all three? He is the perfect balance of power. Indeed, He is the power. The LORD: He is the Judge, He is the Lawgiver, and He is the King.

Isaiah 33:22 goes on to say, "He will save us." Friend, it is all headed to Jesus. It was all and it is all for Him, for the Lord Jesus Christ. He is the key to the mystery of history.

Not long ago, a young man was taking a philosophy course. He'd studied and studied and headed to class to take his final exam. On the exam, his philosophy professor showed a sense of humor and tested his students to see how well they could think. The final examination was just one word: *Why?* The student—the young man—thought for a while. Then he wrote one word down on his exam, and walked out. His answer: *Because.*

I would add two more words if given the same question of *Why?* Because of Jesus. He is the mystery of history. Why is it all made? "All things were created through Him and for Him." And history has a date with deity.

JESUS RECONCILES THE FALLEN

Not only does Jesus reveal the Father and not only does Jesus rule the future, but Jesus also reconciles the fallen. That's why He came. Read Colossians 1:18-20 once again:

> And He is the head of the body, the church, who is
> the beginning, the firstborn from the dead, that in all

things He may have the preeminence. For it pleased the Father that in Him all the fullness should dwell, and by Him to reconcile all things to Himself, by Him, whether things on earth or things in heaven, having made peace through the blood of His cross.

This is so wonderful. This Jesus who declares the Father is the same Jesus who dominates the future. Equally important, this Jesus who delivers the fallen is the same One who reconciles God and man. You see, Christians are not just nicer people. They're not just people who give intellectual assent to certain doctrinal things. There is so much more that happens when we come to Christ.

In Colossians 1, Paul says, "Look, He is the One who made everything. He made it all. It all belongs to Him. And yet He hung naked on a cross." Think of it. "God, the mighty Maker, died for man, the creature's sin."[16]

The One who made every seed, every limb, and every tree also died on a tree. The One who made the oceans, and the fountains, and the rivers and the streams says, "I thirst." The One who flung that sun out into space is the One who was blistered by the noonday sun. His death and His deity are wound together. Other people have died, but it is His death that makes His deity meaningful. And it is His death that makes His deity knowable.

When Jesus created the universe, He did it with His Word. He said: "Let there be," and there was. Expressly, universes sprang from His fingertips. And, as He saved us, it took every drop of His blood. He didn't have to do that. Yet, He died for you and for me.

Truly, He's the Son of God revealed in the pages of His Holy Word. Moreover, He's the One that took my sin, your sin, and our sin to the cross. On the cross, He made peace. And on His cross, He took sinful man with one hand, holy God with the other hand, and reconciled the two.

The story is told of a woman who was dying. The doctors didn't know who she was—she was a Jane Doe. She was in a hospital, without any friends or family. So, the hospital staff called for a minister. As the minister came into her room, he bent down and whispered in her ear, "They say you're dying. Have you made peace with God?" She shook her head negatively.

The doctors and minister huddled a while and came back, wanting to press the point. The minister asked, "Dear lady, you're dying. Don't you think you need to make peace with God?" She shook her head again in the negative. They deliberated and came back a third time and said, "You need to make peace with God." She said, "No, I don't. I am resting in the peace that Jesus has already made."

Correspondingly, you and I cannot make peace with God. Jesus made peace for us with the blood of His cross. Our response is to enter into that peace by faith and trust in the Lord Jesus.

CONCLUSION

What is the bottom line? "That in all things He may have the preeminence." Does He have pre-eminence in your life?

Ellis A. Fuller was a great preacher of yesterday. Fuller had a girlfriend that he loved and wanted to marry. In proposing to her, he simply said, "Would you be willing to take second place in my life?"[17]

Jesus is, and always will be, number one. My wife knows that she's not number one in my life. She knows she's number two, and she'd much rather have it that way because she knows that I love her better when Jesus takes first place.

Does Jesus Christ have the preeminence in your life? If not, what right do you have to call yourself a Christian? "That in all things," everything, "He should have the preeminence."

Who is Jesus? He's the Jesus of this the Bible, and He reveals the Father. Likewise, Jesus is the image of the invisible God who is Spirit—invisible, unfathomable, unapproachable. How are we going to know God? Only through Jesus.

ENDNOTES

1. "The Search for Jesus: Peter Jennings Reporting." ABC NEWS, 2000.

2. Donald, Pastor. "It's All About Jesus Christ." *www.mtzionofbeaufort. com/hp_wordpress/wp-content/uploads/2019/12/Newsletter-December-2019.pdf.*

3. Blanchard, John. "Why Jesus Came." *byfaithonline.com*, 22 Dec. 2009, byfaithonline.com/why-jesus-came/.

4. "List of Religious Populations." *Wikipedia*, Wikimedia Foundation, 9 Feb. 2020, en.wikipedia.org/wiki/List_of_religious_populations.

5. "SimplyScott." *December 2010*, 21 Dec. 2010, simplyscotts.blogspot. com/2010/12/.

6. "Adrian Rogers: Who Is Jesus?" *The Daily Hatch*, 15 Sept. 2019, thedailyhatch.org/2019/09/11/adrian-rogers-who-is-jesus/.

7. Culbertson, Howard. *Responses to Jehovah's Witnesses (Page 1)*, home. snu.edu/~hculbert/jehovah.htm.

8. "Irreducible Complexity: The Challenge to the Darwinian Evolutionary Explanations of Many Biochemical Structures." *IDEA Center*, www.ideacenter.org/contentmgr/showdetails.php/id/840.

9. *UCSB Science Line*, scienceline.ucsb.edu/getkey.php?key=3926.

10. "The Genetic Basics: What Are Genes and What Do They Do? - A Revolution in Progress: Human Genetics and Medical Research." *National Institutes of Health*, U.S. Department of Health and Human Services, history. nih.gov/exhibits/genetics/sect1a.htm.

11. Kuhn, Bradley. *What's So Special About Me?* May 17, 2008.

12. Redd, Nola Taylor. "How Fast Does Light Travel?: The Speed of Light." *Space.com*, Space, 7 Mar. 2018, www.space.com/15830-light-speed. html.

13. Temming, Maria. "How Many Stars Are There in the Universe?" *Sky & Telescope*, 15 Aug. 2018, www.skyandtelescope.com/astronomy-resources/ how-many-stars-are-there/.

14. https://translate.yandex.com/translator/English-Greek

15. "Reincarnation." *Wikipedia*, Wikimedia Foundation, 19 Feb. 2020, en.wikipedia.org/wiki/Reincarnation.

16. Watts, Isaac WattsIsaac, et al. "Alas, and Did My Savior Bleed." *Hymnary.org*, hymnary.org/text/alas_and_did_my_savior_bleed.

17. Hanbury, Aaron. "The Life and Legacy of Ellis A. Fuller – The Southern Baptist Theological Seminary." *SBTS*, 23 Nov. 2010, www.sbts.edu/ blog/2010/11/23/the-life-and-legacy-of-ellis-a-fuller/.

HOW TO ENJOY THE PRESENCE OF GOD

EXODUS 32-33

"When you have the presence of God, you need nothing more, but you should settle for nothing less."
—Adrian Rogers

I f you were to give a definition of worship, what would it be? Is worship enjoying God? I believe it is. Indeed, I think that worship is enjoying the presence of God. And that's what this chapter is all about—how to enjoy the presence of God.

The longer I live, the more I study, the more I experience, and the more I realize that this is the bottom line, the highest good, the most wonderful fulfillment—to know God intimately and to enjoy Him personally.

Now let me ask you a question. Do you know God personally? I'm not asking if you know about Him. You might know about George Washington. Instead, I'm asking if you know God personally.

Is He today, this moment, in your heart and life, a bright, living, vital reality? If so, then you know the deepest pleasure. You have fulfilled the deepest need. And, you have attained that for which you were created, to know God personally. Because, you see, worship is enjoying the presence of God. You need nothing more. You should settle for nothing less.

Honestly, there are many Christians today who do not have the conscious presence of God in their lives. They show up at church, they sing the songs, they may muster an, "Amen," but there is a deadness, a dryness, and a void in their life. Consider some of the most frightening words in all of the Bible. They're found here in Exodus 33:1-3,

> Then the LORD said to Moses, "Depart and go up from here, you and the people whom you have brought out of the land of Egypt, to the land of which I swore to Abraham, Isaac, and Jacob, saying, 'To your descendants I will give it.' And I will send My Angel before you, and I will drive out the Canaanite and the Amorite and the Hittite and the Perizzite and the Hivite and the Jebusite. Go up to a land flowing with milk and honey; for I will not go up in your midst, lest I consume you on the way, for you are a stiff-necked people."

What are the frightening words? God says, "I'm not going with you. I will not go up in your midst."

The Jewish people, the sons of Abraham, are out in the wilderness. God has given them a covenant and a promise. And, they are headed toward the Promised Land. However, in the middle of their journey, they terribly sin against God.

God says, "All right, I promise that I'm going to give you the land, a land that flows with milk and honey. I will give you an angel escort into the land. And when you get there, the land will flow with milk and honey. But I am not going with you."

Now that's frightening—to have success, to have possessions, to have protection, but not to have the presence of the Lord. "I'm going to give you an angel to take care of you," He says. In other words, God tells them that He will get them into the land but not personally go with them. That would be like two people getting married and then living in separate bedrooms.

Don't settle for success without the Lord. Don't settle for even "seeming" success without the Lord. As a matter of fact, George McDonald once said, "In whatever a man does without God, he will either fail miserably or succeed even more miserably."[18]

Continuing on in Exodus 33, let's get a little background. Moses had gone up to Mount Sinai to receive the Ten Commandments and instructions for the Tabernacle. While Moses was gone, Aaron, his brother, led the people into a revolt against Almighty God. In summary, Aaron said, "We don't know what's happened to Moses. He's been up there a long time. Maybe he's never coming back. We need some guidance, we need some help, and we need some leadership. Give me your bracelets and your earrings, and we will make a golden calf. We will worship that golden calf." So, that's what the people did.

Go back to Exodus 32:4 to pick up this part of the story.

> And he received the gold from their hand, and he fashioned it with an engraving tool, and made a molded calf. Then they said, "This is your god, O Israel, that brought you out of the land of Egypt!" So when Aaron saw it, he built an altar before it. And Aaron made a proclamation and said, "Tomorrow is a feast to the LORD." Then they rose early on the next day, offered burnt offerings, and brought peace offerings; and the people sat down to eat and drink, and rose up to play. And the LORD said to Moses, "Go, get down! For your people whom you brought out of the land of Egypt have corrupted themselves. They have turned aside quickly out of the way which I commanded them. They have made themselves a molded calf, and worshiped it and sacrificed to it, and said, 'This is your god, O Israel, that brought you out of the land of Egypt!'" And the LORD said to Moses, "I have seen this people, and indeed it is a stiff-necked people! Now therefore, let Me alone, that My wrath may burn hot against them and I may consume them. And I will make of you a great nation." (vv. 4-10)

When Moses comes down off the mountain, he sees this charade, orgy, and feast. In the name of worship, they were naked, committing immorality, and doing horrible things while dancing around a golden calf. Truly, Moses is so grieved that he takes the Ten Commandments and throws them to the ground and breaks those tablets of stone. Then he takes the golden calf, and has it ground into powder; he mixes the powder with water and makes the people drink it. Indeed, their greatest delight has become their greatest displeasure.

In the midst of this crisis, Moses goes to God to intercede. He puts himself in the place of the people and cries out on their behalf. This section of the story is found in Exodus 32:30-32.

> Now it came to pass on the next day that Moses said to the people, "You have committed a great sin. So now I will go up to the LORD; perhaps I can make atonement for your sin." Then Moses returned to the LORD and said, "Oh, these people have committed a great sin, and have made for themselves a god of gold! Yet now, if You will forgive their sin—but if not, I pray, blot me out of Your book which You have written."

In Exodus 33:1, we read God's response to Moses's pleading: "Then the Lord said to Moses, "Depart and go up from here, you and the people whom you have brought out of the land of Egypt, to the land of which I swore to Abraham, Isaac, and Jacob, saying, 'To your descendants I will give it.'" In other words, God pledges not to destroy the people. For Moses' sake, God will send an angel to protect them and fulfill His promise to them. But, God will not be personally going with them the rest of their journey.

There's a lesson to be learned from this story: Do not settle for protection; do not settle for provision; do not settle for a Promised Land without the presence of God. Just don't do it. When you have the presence of God, you need nothing more, but you should settle for nothing less.

There are a lot of people today who have no joy or sense of purpose. They are secure in the promise of heaven, but their lives on earth are empty. In total honesty, they would have to admit that they do not enjoy the manifest presence of God in their lives. They have His protection, His provision, and His promise, but they do not have the sweet presence of God in their lives.

Don't think that just because you have His provision and protection that you're right with God. Yes, you may be on your way to Heaven, but you're certainly traveling there second class. May I remind you that even a nonbeliever has certain provisions: food and air and clothes and houses? Could you and I become so preoccupied with getting provision and protection that we fail to have His presence?

Israel, however, knew better than that, and thank God that they did. Look in Exodus 33:4: "And when the people heard this bad news, they mourned, and no one put on his ornaments." They understood the reality of having the gifts without the Giver. Certainly, it is empty to have blessings without the Blesser and to have the promise without the Provider and the manifest presence of God. So, what made Israel different from the other nations? It was God's presence in the midst of them.

Is the presence of God, the Shekinah glory of God, this moment very real to you, or are you just simply fulfilling your duty sitting in church on Sundays? As you listen to worship music, is your heart thrilled and filled with the presence of God? If not, this message is for you, because worship is indeed enjoying the presence of God. In your life, it could be that you once knew the glory of God, and now that glory has departed or faded. Possibly the glory of God is gone, and your life has become dry.

What caused God to withdraw His manifested presence from His people? There are four things that robbed Israel and will rob you of the manifested presence of God in your life.

DIRECT DISOBEDIENCE

First; the people directly disobeyed God. In Exodus 32:7-8 we read,

And the LORD said to Moses, "Go, get down! For your people whom you brought out of the land of Egypt have corrupted themselves. They have turned aside quickly out of the way which I commanded them. They have made themselves a molded calf, and worshiped it and sacrificed to it, and said, 'This is your god, O Israel, that brought you out of the land of Egypt!'"

Do you know the problem with a lot of people? They have walked down a church aisle, confessed faith in the Lord Jesus Christ, subscribed to the authentic doctrines of the church, followed the Lord in believer's baptism, but they do not have the presence of God. They don't even have the assurance of their salvation.

It's the Holy Spirit's job to confirm your salvation. It's the Holy Spirit of God that gives you the assurance that you belong to Him. First John 4:13 tells us, "By this we know that we abide in Him, and He in us, because He has given us of His Spirit."

Could anything be clearer than this? Read it one more time, "By this we know that we abide in Him, and He in us, because He has given us of His Spirit." Similarly, Romans 8:16 gives us this promise: "The Spirit Himself bears witness with our spirit that we are children of God." It is clear that it is the work of the Holy Spirit to give us the assurance that we belong to the Lord Jesus Christ. Both the Apostle Paul and John echo the promise that because of the Holy Spirit, we have the assurance of our salvation.

You may ask, what does this all have to do with the manifested presence of God? And how does this relate to the disobedience that we read about in Exodus 33? Simply this: when you knowingly, willingly, with eyes wide open, disobey God, you grieve the Holy Spirit of God. That's the reason the Bible says, "And do not grieve the Holy Spirit of God, by whom you were sealed for the day of redemption" (Ephesians 4:30).

Did you know that you can only grieve somebody who loves you? For example, the neighbors' kids may irritate you, but your own children will grieve you. What's the difference? *Grieve* is a love word. The Holy Spirit of God loves you, but you can grieve Him when you disobey the commandments of God. Again, the Bible says in 1 Thessalonians 5:19, "Do not quench the Spirit."

Do you know what the word *quench* means? It means to pour cold water on a fire. The Holy Spirit is like a gentle dove;

the Holy Spirit is like a glowing ember. You can frighten away that dove and you can pour water on that ember. The Bible says in Ephesians 5:18, "Be filled with the Spirit," then it says, "Grieve not, quench not." In summary, we are to be filled, grieve not, and quench not.

Who is it that manifests the life of God in you? The Holy Spirit of God is like what the pillar of cloud and the pillar of fire was for the Israelites. Correspondingly, He is the Shekinah glory of God, the manifested presence of God in your life!

In the event that you willfully, knowingly, deliberately disobey God, you grieve the Spirit; you quench the Spirit. When you quench the Spirit, God ceases to be real to you. You can even wonder, "Am I saved?" I've met many people who doubt their salvation. They may be saved, but they are living in direct disobedience to God. As a result, they do not enjoy the manifested presence of God.

Consider John 14:21. It's one of the key verses about enjoying the presence of God. In this verse, Jesus says, "He who has My commandments and keeps them, it is he who loves Me. And he who loves Me will be loved by My Father, and I will love him and manifest Myself to him." When people truly love God, they obey Him and live for Him.

A man talked to his pastor and said, "Pastor, I don't know what's wrong with me, but God is not real to me anymore. I don't have any joy; the presence of God is not real in my heart, in my life, like it used to be." This wise pastor asked him a direct question, "Is there any known sin in your life? Any unconfessed, unrepented sin in your life?"

In that moment, that man said, "Well, Pastor, let me tell you something. I used to bring a tithe of my income to God. I believe the Word of God when the Bible taught that we are to bring all the tithe into the storehouse. But," he said, "some time ago I got the idea that perhaps God didn't need that as much as I needed it."

The pastor said, "Do you know what you've done? You've begun to steal from God." He said, "Sir, you wouldn't put your hand in the offering plate when it is passed and take some money out that other people had given to God. Would you steal from the offering plate? Malachi says, 'When a man is not faithful in stewardship, he's robbing God.'"

Then, the pastor went on to say, "What do you think God does when one of His children behaves like this? Do you think God will say, 'My child has chosen to disobey Me. He's stealing from Me. And, he cannot trust Me to take care of his needs. Nor will he obey Me. Now this week I think I will bless him with even more financial resources, and I'll make My presence very real to him.'"

Do you think God would do that? Will God say, "I'm going to display Myself to this man; I'm going to give him a deeper sense of My presence and My approval." No. This is not how God works. God does not bless disobedience and willful sin.

Let's look back at the story in Exodus. Do you know who it was that encouraged these people to disobey God and lose the manifest presence of God? It was Aaron. Do you know who Aaron was? Aaron was a priest, a religious leader. Even today, there will always be plenty of people who will give you a reason, an excuse to disobey God. And it may even be a religious leader. They'll lead you into an unscriptural marriage, immorality, or a transgression of the commandments of God. They will even tell you that the sin is okay because times have changed.

But I remind you one more time that Jesus says in John 14:21, "He who has My commandments and keeps them, it is he who loves Me. And he who loves Me will be loved by My Father, and I will love him and manifest Myself to him."

Can I ask you a question? Have you rejected a direct command of God? Are you living right now in disobedience to a known command of God? If you are, there's no reason that I can think of in all of the Bible where you ought to have a sense of the manifest presence of God. God loves you too much to manifest Himself to you in glory and yet have you live in disobedience.

DIVIDED DEVOTION

Consider a second question, do you have any divided devotion to God? Not only direct disobedience, but divided devotion. Read the words of Exodus 32:4, "And he received the gold from their hand, and he fashioned it with an engraving tool, and made a molded calf. Then they said, 'This is your god, O Israel, that brought you out of the land of Egypt!'"

Now what had these people done? They had divided their devotion. Although they claimed to be Israel—the people of God—they had made a golden calf and worshipped it. Even more, rather than trusting Almighty God, they began to trust the work of their hands. This was idolatry. The Bible teaches us that when people make an idol, they become like the idol. First the man molds the idol, and then the idol molds the man. What is an idol? An idol is just a magnified sinner. A man takes his own ideas, makes an idol, and then begins to worship it. Ultimately, he ends up worshipping himself.

Is there a golden calf in your life? An idol? Truly, anything that you love more than God is an idol. Anything that you fear more than God is an idol. Anything that you serve more than God is an idol. Anything that you trust more than God is an idol.

G.K. Chesterton said it well: "When we cease to worship the true God, it is not that we worship nothing; it is that we'll worship anything."[19] In your own life, is there any direct disobedience, any divided devotion, or anything that you love more, fear more, serve more, or trust more than Almighty God? If there is, it's no wonder that God's presence is not real in your heart and in your life.

Moreover, if the glory of God is gone in your life, if God is not real to you, answer this question: Is there anyone or anything that takes precedence over God in your life? God doesn't want a place in your life. God despises prominence in your life. Indeed, God demands preeminence in your life. He will take nothing less.

God's throne is not a duplex. Is there anything that is a greater controlling factor of your behavior than God? Is there a relationship that means more to you than your relationship with the Lord? Is there treasure that means more to you? Is there anything that gets more of your attention than Almighty God? Then, it should not come as a surprise to you that because of that golden calf in your life, God says, "I'm not going with you. I'll not be in the midst of you. I just won't do it."

DISPLACED DEPENDENCE

Let's consider a third question that you might ponder if God is not real in your life: Do you detect any displaced dependence? Look again at Exodus 32:7-8:

> And the LORD said to Moses, "Go, get down! For your people whom you brought out of the land of Egypt have corrupted themselves. They have turned aside quickly out of the way which I commanded them. They have made themselves a molded calf, and worshiped it and sacrificed to it, and said, 'This is your god, O Israel, that brought you out of the land of Egypt!'"

In this story, the people began to put their dependence on the work of their own hands. As they began to worship the golden calf, they no longer depended on Almighty God that brought them through the Red Sea. Do you know what happens when you and I stop depending on God? When God gives us a victory, and we give the glory to something else or someone else other than God, we begin to lose the presence of God.

Let me illustrate. Consider the amazing church buildings that we are privileged to worship in each week. The walls are saturated with prayer and these carpets are stained with the tears of God's people. This place is the place of prayer, faith, and obedience that was built for us.

But suppose—even with all of these blessings from God—we start taking credit for our church. We thank the building committee and all who gave money. As we look around, we begin to take credit for our church and all of the wonderful things that are happening. It is in this moment that God takes off. His presence will leave the building.

When the people in Moses' day began to give credit to the golden calf and give this false god honor, God wanted nothing to do with them. He would not go with them any longer.

During the Persian Gulf War, George H. W. Bush was the president of the United States. As our nation came up against what we thought was an implacable foe, Saddam Hussein, many of us were glued to the television. I can remember staying up at night and watching those patriot missiles fly in the air. It was a time of great concern and anxiety for all of us.[20]

Do you remember what happened in our churches? Sunday morning attendance was up twenty-five percent. People across the land filled the churches. Even more, they cried out to God and begged Him for protection and for the end of the looming conflict in the Middle East. As SCUD missiles flew into Israel, fears mounted over how Israel might retaliate. Undoubtedly, there was more prayer during those days than had been uttered in a long time in our country.

Not surprisingly, God answered our prayers. And, as soon as Desert Storm was over, do you know what we did? We began to give credit to our generals, our leaders, our strategies, and our patriot missiles. What's more, we failed to give God the glory. We failed to have national revival. We failed to continue to follow God and love God and serve God. Even worse, we took a deep nosedive away from God and into sin as our nation has never seen before.

Think about it. Never did we have a more glorious victory. Never did God protect a people and let us get out of a mess as He did in this situation. But then we made a golden calf and took credit for our own victory. Sadly, we failed to give God the credit and the glory for protecting us from war and destruction.

There's a great lesson here. When God gives you a blessing, is good to you, and brings you through the storm, you must give Him glory. If you begin to give credit where credit is not due and fail to give God the glory, is it any wonder that His presence is not real in your life?

DETERMINED DEFIANCE

Let's consider one last question: Is there any determined defiance in our lives? Look at Exodus 32:9: "'And the LORD said to Moses, "I have seen this people, and indeed it is a stiff-necked people!"' What does this mean? *Stiff-necked* is the opposite of being soft and pliable. To be *stiff-necked* is to be like a horse who bucks, fights, and will not let you lead him.[21]

If God speaks to you about what He wants you to do, then obey Him. Has God told you there's somebody He wants you to witness to? Has God been laying somebody on your heart and you're not witnessing to that person? No wonder God's not real to you. Has God been putting some impulse in your heart to serve in your church—perhaps to work in the preschool, the nursery, the youth group, parking lot, or kitchen?

Are you doing what God has prompted you to do? Has God been laying on your heart something He wants you to give, some sacrificial gift? Has God been leading you to apologize to someone and make things right? Has God been telling you there's a relationship that you're in that you need to break off? Has God been speaking to your heart and calling you into missions or full-time Christian service? Has God been telling you to do something, go somewhere, be something, give something? And you have said, "No." Then, you have had a stiff neck.

God wants to be real in your life. And, I pray that He will be real to you. Prayerfully read once more the words of Jesus in John 14:21: "He who has My commandments and keeps them, it is he who loves Me. And he who loves Me will be loved by My Father, and I will love him and manifest Myself to him."

Why not pray this prayer right now:

Lord Jesus, I want You to manifest Yourself to me personally. If I have disobeyed You willingly, forgive me. Lord, if I love anything more than You, from now on, You will be number one in my life. Lord, if I'm trusting the work of my own hands or my own ingenuity, I quit it right now. Lord, if there's anything You want me to do, I'm available, here I am. Lord, as I go, go with me. Father, I pray in the name of Jesus that You'll seal this to my heart. Amen.

ENDNOTES

18. *Our Daily Bread,* odb.org/2013/06/28/miserable-success/.

19. "A Quote by G.K. Chesterton." *Goodreads,* Goodreads, www.goodreads.com/quotes/44015-when-men-choose-not-to-believe-in-god-they-do.

20. History.com Editors. "Persian Gulf War." *History.com,* A&E Television Networks, 9 Nov. 2009, www.history.com/topics/middle-east/persian-gulf-war.

21. "Stiff-Necked Definition and Meaning - Bible Dictionary." *Bible Study Tools,* www.biblestudytools.com/dictionary/stiff-necked/.

THREE STRIKES AND YOU'RE OUT

MARK 10:17-27

"Faith is not merely nodding a head to a series of theological facts about Jesus. It is enthroning Jesus."
—Adrian Rogers

There is a problem, a real problem today in our churches. People attend church, they listen to sermons, they join churches, but they are never radically, dramatically, eternally changed. They have religion, but they've never met God.

Many churches today are filled with baptized pagans. They have been vaccinated with a mild form of Christianity, but they've never caught the real disease. Indeed, the church may be full, but the people are often quite empty. Each week, they show up and go through the motions and try to live a good life, but they have not truly found new life. They've never been converted.

Now with that in mind, I want you to look at a passage of Scripture in Mark 10:17-27:

Now as He was going out on the road, one came running, knelt before Him, and asked Him, "Good Teacher, what shall I do that I may inherit eternal life?" So Jesus said to him, "Why do you call Me good? No one is good but One, that is, God. You know the commandments: 'Do not commit adultery,' 'Do not murder,' 'Do not steal,' 'Do not bear false witness,' 'Do not defraud,' 'Honor your father and your mother.'" And he answered and said to Him, "Teacher, all these things I have kept from my youth." Then Jesus, looking at him, loved him, and said to him, "One thing you lack: Go your way, sell whatever you have and give to the poor, and you will have treasure in heaven; and come, take up the cross, and follow Me." But he was sad at this word, and went away sorrowful, for he had great possessions. Then Jesus looked around and said to His disciples, "How hard it is for those who have riches to enter the kingdom of God!" And the disciples were astonished at His words. But Jesus answered again and said to them, "Children, how hard it is for those who trust in riches to enter the kingdom of God! It is easier for a camel to go through the eye of a needle than for a rich man to enter the kingdom of God." And they were greatly astonished, saying among themselves, "Who then can be saved?" But Jesus looked at them and said, "With men it is impossible, but not with God; for with God all things are possible."

In considering the truths of this passage, there are four points I'd like you to consider.

PROUD PEOPLE AT THEIR BEST ARE SINNERS AT THEIR WORST

First, I'd like to note that proud people at their best are sinners at their worst. Now you may not see it on the surface, but the man in Mark 10 was quite proud of his achievements and accomplishments.

Outwardly he had much to be proud of. As a matter of fact, outwardly he had very much that we would admire.

First of all, he was eager. The Bible says he came running to meet with Jesus. He was full of the strength and the vigor of youth. And I like enthusiasm. I know there are some folks who come to church on Sunday morning wearing a sign hanging around their necks that says, "Please do not disturb." Truly, some of you are not enthusiastic about the things of God. But the man in our story had enthusiasm; I love people with vibrant enthusiasm.

Not only was he enthusiastic, he was also humble. The man came and knelt before Jesus. Although Jesus was a peasant prophet from Galilee, this rich, young ruler knelt before Him. Despite the fact that he had position, power and prestige at a young age, he humbled himself before Jesus.

Sadly, there are a lot of people who are going to go to hell because of their abominable pride. They don't want anybody to know that they have any needs in their life. When invited to come to Christ, they don't realize their great need for Him. Instead, they look around to see who else might need to accept Christ. Pride keeps them from the Savior and from salvation.

A third great trait about the rich, young ruler was his discernment. He knew there was something about Jesus that was different. Indeed, he said to Jesus, "Good Teacher, what shall I do that I may inherit eternal life?" (v. 17). This young man knew worth and he knew goodness when he saw it. Today, in our churches, there are a lot of people who cannot even discern goodness, even in the Lord Jesus Christ. Our pews are filled with cynics who know the price of everything and the value of nothing.

In addition, this young ruler had his mind on spiritual things. He didn't say, "What must I do to make a killing in the stock market? What must I do to have pleasure and ease?" He asked this question: "What must I do to inherit eternal life?"

Can I ask you a question: what are you interested in? Most of us are not interested in going to Heaven or trying to miss hell. Instead, we are interested in tomorrow and the hum-drum issues of life. Are we missing the most vital question in life because we are entangled in the mundane cares of this world?

Another great trait of the rich young ruler was His moral purity. Jesus said, "You know the commandments" (v. 19). In fact, the young man told Jesus, "Teacher, all these things I have kept from my youth" (v. 20). Outwardly, this young man did not steal, commit adultery, or lie. Further, he wasn't taking God's name in vain and he kept the Sabbath.

This young man honored his father and his mother and would have made a wonderful neighbor. He was a kind of a man you could trust to watch your house while you went on vacation. Also, he was morally clean—the kind of man that you would not be afraid for your children to be around. Trustworthy and honest, he'd be a fabulous business partner.

One other admirable trait about this rich young ruler was that he was incredibly successful. If he had joined the average church in America, they would have welcomed him in and made him the church treasurer. His accomplishments were commendable, and he was quite impressive.

But Jesus did not praise or flatter him. Instead, Jesus seems to treat him rather harshly. Look in Mark 10:18, and see what the Lord says: "Why do you call Me good? No one is good but One, that is, God." In this conversation Jesus is teaching this young man that he is not good. No one is good but God.

Also, Jesus told this young man that He Himself is God. You can't just tip your hat and not bow your knee to Jesus. Jesus is God. And, if Jesus in not God, Jesus is not good. How do I know? Jesus Christ Himself said so. Jesus said, "No one is good but One, that is, God," (v. 18). In this one sentence, Jesus basically says, "I am God and you're a sinner. No one is good but One, that is, God."

Another passage that speaks to this same truth is Romans 3:10-12: "As it is written: 'There is none righteous, no, not one; there is none who understands; there is none who seeks after God. They have all turned aside; they have together become unprofitable; there is none who does good, no, not one.'"

The truth of these words impact us all. None of us are righteous. Not even me. Not even you. Nobody has ever been saved until he has seen that he is a poor, lost sinner in the sight of a righteous and a holy God. The young man is talking about eternal life, and Jesus shocks him and says, "No one is good but One, that is, God."

In our world today, there are people who join churches and act like they're doing God a wild favor. Although they are spiritual or somewhat religious, they have never truly seen the holiness of God. Furthermore, they don't see their own sinfulness and the wrath of God against their sin.

Consider the words of Exodus 34:6-7 and the character of God:

And the LORD passed before him and proclaimed, "The LORD, the LORD God, merciful and gracious, longsuffering, and abounding in goodness and truth, keeping mercy for thousands, forgiving iniquity and transgression and sin, by no means clearing the guilty, visiting the iniquity of the fathers upon the children and the children's children to the third and the fourth generation."

Do you understand what this passage means? It means that God is love and God is justice. In our society today, we hear so much about the love of God. God is love; that is true. Absolutely, He is a God of mercy. But that's not ALL of the truth. Indeed, if you take part of the truth and try to make that part of truth all of the truth, then that part of the truth becomes an untruth.

Certainly, God is a God of mercy; God does forgive iniquity. What's more, the Bible says that God will: "by no means clearing the guilty," (v. 7). Don't think that somehow when you stand before God, God is going to look at your sin and say, "Oh, that's alright. Your sin is okay."

This is not possible! For if God were to clear the guilty, God would Himself become guilty. God would topple from His throne of holiness. If God were to overlook sin or bypass sin, then God becomes a sinner. Do you know what they say in a court of law? "The judge is condemned, when the criminal is acquitted."[22] God Himself would become a sinner if God excused our sin.

What is Jesus teaching the young ruler in this story? Jesus is teaching that proud people—at their best—are really sinners at their worst. There are no good people. Jesus said, "No one is good but One, that is, God" (Mark 10:18). No man, no woman, no boy, no girl has been truly converted until he sees himself as a sinner in the sight of a righteous and a holy God.

Now why did I say that good men at their best are sinners at their worst? Why didn't I say that bad men are sinners at their worst? Because the worst sin of all sins is human goodness. This is especially true when human goodness becomes a substitute for the new birth. The worst form of badness is human goodness. Jesus said that prostitutes and crooked tax collectors were going to Heaven before the Pharisees because they had substituted their self-righteousness for God's mercy.

No matter how well a person may live, they are not good apart from Christ. None is good except God. Proud people at their best are sinners at their worst.

GOD'S PERFECT LAW CONDEMNS OUR SINFUL PRIDE

There's a second truth we see in Mark 10:17-27. God's perfect law condemns our sinful pride. Read Mark 10:19-21 again.

> You know the commandments: 'Do not commit adultery,' 'Do not murder,' 'Do not steal,' 'Do not bear false witness,' 'Do not defraud,' 'Honor your father and your mother.'" And he answered and said to Him, "Teacher, all these things I have kept from my youth." Then Jesus, looking at him, loved him, and said to him, "One thing you lack: Go your way, sell whatever you have and give to the poor, and you will have treasure in heaven; and come, take up the cross, and follow Me."

If God is a holy God, He will have holy laws. This is as certain as the fact that night follows day. Jesus is not teaching salvation by commandment-keeping. Rather, He is teaching just the opposite. The Bible teaches that you're not saved by keeping the commandments. But yet this young man asked in Mark 10:17, "Good Teacher, what shall I do that I may inherit eternal life?" And Jesus begins to refer him to the commandments.

Commandment-keeping has never saved anybody. Galatians 2:16 tells us, "knowing that a man is not justified by the works of the law but by faith in Jesus Christ, even we have believed in Christ Jesus, that we might be justified by faith in Christ and not by the works of the law; for by the works of the law no flesh shall be justified."

The law, the Ten Commandments, cannot save anybody. However, while the Ten Commandments do not save you, they are an essential element in evangelism and salvation. What is the purpose of the law? Why does God give us the law? To let us know that we're sinners!

Consider the words of Romans 3:20: "Therefore by the deeds of the law no flesh will be justified in His sight, for by the law is the knowledge of sin." God gave us the law to let us know that we're sinners. And Jesus is using the law in this passage to teach this young man that he's a sinner. Using the commandments, He shows this young ruler that He needs a Savior.

When my wife Joyce and I were on our honeymoon, we were driving near Daytona Beach. As we entered a small town, I was driving about 45 miles per hour and attracted the attention of a policeman. He pulled me over and said, "Young man, you're breaking the speed limit."

I said, "Sir, I'm not breaking the speed limit; I'm only doing about 45 miles an hour."

He said, "The limit here is 35 miles an hour."

I said, "Well, why don't you put up a sign that says the speed limit is 35 miles an hour?"

He said, "We put one up."

I said, "I didn't see it."

"Well," he said, "it's back there about a mile. I suggest that you go turn around and go back and take a look at it."

So, I did. And he let me go.

It was by the law that I had the knowledge of my sin. Similarly, God has His commandments. So many times we're just driving along thinking we're doing quite all right. But you see, God gives us the holy law so that we can see that we're sinners in the sight of a righteous and a holy God.

After all, what is sin? There're many definitions of sin. Let me give you one of the best in the Bible. It's in 1 John 3:4: "Whoever commits sin also commits lawlessness, and sin is lawlessness." That's what sin is. Sin is just breaking God's law.

Now, why did Jesus give this young man an illustration? Why did Jesus talk to this young man about keeping the commandments? I'll tell you why. God's grace will mean nothing to a man until, first of all, he sees himself a sinner in the sight of a righteous and holy God. God gives us the law so that we might see that we are sinners. Remember this: "for by the law is the knowledge of sin" (Romans 3:20).

Often, little children want to join the church and be baptized. Their parents will ask me if they are ready to be saved. I often will tell parents that the key to salvation readiness is the realization that they are sinners. When children recognize that God is holy and they are not, then they are ready to give their hearts to Christ. The same is true for all of us.

In other words, we don't have to have a Ph.D. in sin or theology in order to be saved. Once we see ourselves as sinners in the sight of a righteous and a holy God, we are ready. And, as has been noted, the law is given that we might see in the sight of God that we are sinners. Luke 5:32 reminds us of Jesus' words, "have not come to call the righteous, but sinners, to repentance."

The law doesn't save us, but the law gets us ready to be saved. So many people don't have any concept of salvation because they've never seen the absolute holiness of God. The scripture reminds us, "No one is good but One, that is, God" (Mark 10:18). When we are wounded by God's law, then we are ready for the healing balm of salvation.

Looking back to the story, we notice that the rich young ruler had a superficial knowledge of the law. And Jesus said, "You know the commandments?" (v. 19).

He said, "Well, I've kept them from my law, from my youth up" (v. 20).

In Romans 7:14, the Bible says, "For we know that the law is spiritual, but I am carnal, sold under sin." Consider also this truth: the law is spiritual. That is, everything that you do in your outward life may look all right, but the law is spiritual. It deals with the heart.

For example, Jesus said in Matthew 5:27-28, "You have heard that it was said to those of old, 'You shall not commit adultery.' But I say to you that whoever looks at a woman to lust for her has already committed adultery with her in his heart."

Some people will say that they have never committed adultery, but God may have written down *adultery* in His records in Heaven. The law says, "You shall not murder." But Jesus said: "...whoever is angry with his brother without a cause shall be in danger of the judgment" (Matthew 5:21-22).

As the conversation progressed in the passage, the young man told Jesus that He had kept the commandments and behaved with honor. But Jesus took a scalpel and cut to the heart of the matter when He said, "One thing you lack: Go your way, sell whatever you have and give to the poor, and you will have treasure in heaven; and come, take up the cross, and follow Me" (Mark 10:21).

These words deeply impacted the young ruler. For this young man had an idol in his life.

His god was gold. His creed was greed. Although he thought he had kept the whole law, he had actually broken the entire law.

Similarly, on another occasion, a lawyer came to Jesus and he said, "Teacher, which is the great commandment in the law?" (Matthew 22:36).

And Jesus said to him, "You shall love the LORD your God with all your heart, with all your soul, and with all your mind." This is the first and great commandment. And the second is like it: "You shall love your neighbor as yourself," (Matthew 22:37-39). In short conversation, Jesus just summed up the whole Ten Commandments. Love God and love your neighbor. That's what the Ten Commandments are all about.

When Jesus told the rich young ruler what he must do to have eternal life, he wasn't willing to do what he was told. Why not? Number one, he loved his money more than he loved God. And, number two, he loved his money more than he loved his neighbor. Do you see it? In reality, the spirit of this young man had broken all Ten Commandments by failing to do this one thing!

Jesus is not teaching that you can buy your way into Heaven by selling everything you have and giving it to the poor. What Jesus is doing is giving this man a revelation of his heart. In essence, Jesus is showing this man that he's guilty of the sin of covetousness. James 2:10 teaches, "For whoever shall keep the whole law, and yet stumble in one point, he is guilty of all."

To summarize, Jesus is showing this young man the futility of trying to behave himself into Heaven. No one is saved by good behavior or commandment keeping. It's impossible to enter heaven by doing good deeds. That is not how it works. The only way to heaven is through faith in Jesus and true repentance.

NO ONE CAN SERVE TWO MASTERS, BUT HE MUST SERVE ONE

There is a third lesson to be learned from this story. Jesus teaches this young man that no one can serve two masters, but he must serve one. Look back to Mark 10:21-22: "Then Jesus, looking at him, loved him, and said to him, 'One thing you lack: Go your way, sell whatever you have and give to the poor, and you will have treasure in heaven; and come, take up the cross, and follow Me.'"

Why did Jesus make this request to this young man? This young man had an idol in his heart. An idol. A false god. And what was this idol? This idol was his wealth. We see this in Mark 10:23-24: "Then Jesus looked around and said to His disciples, 'How hard it is for those who have riches to enter the kingdom of God!' And the disciples were astonished at His words. But Jesus answered again and said to them, 'Children, how hard it is for those who trust in riches to enter the kingdom of God!'"

In this passage, Jesus is not saying that a rich man can't be saved. Instead, in Mark 10:24, He is referring to those who, "trust in riches to enter the kingdom of God." Whatever a person trusts is his or her god. Anything you love more, serve more, trust more, fear more than almighty God is an idol. Do you see that?

In truth, the rich young ruler had an idol—a false god. Matthew 6:24 reminds us, "No one can serve two masters; for either he will hate the one and love the other, or else he will be loyal to the one and despise the other. You cannot serve God and mammon." You can only serve one master.

In order to have eternal life, this young man needed to repent. Repent of what? Idolatry! 1 Thessalonians 1:9 clarifies: "For they themselves declare concerning us what manner of entry we had to you, and how you turned to God from idols to serve the living and true God."

Just as this young man needed to repent, so do we. In order to go to Heaven, you must turn from any idol you are following and turn to God. This turning is called *repentance*. Honestly, this is where many people miss salvation. They want to add Jesus in with all of the other idols and gods that they serve. But He is not just one more god. He is the only true God. And to know Him personally, you must repent.

Reflect on a few repentance verses with me. First, in Mark 1:15, we read, "The time is fulfilled, and the kingdom of God is at hand. Repent, and believe in the gospel." In Mark 6:12, we are told, "So they went out and preached that people should repent." Acts 2:38 says, "Then Peter said to them, 'Repent, and let every one of you be baptized in the name of Jesus Christ for the remission of sins; and you shall receive the gift of the Holy Spirit.'"

Moreover, in Acts 3:19, we read, "Repent therefore and be converted, that your sins may be blotted out, so that times of refreshing may come from the presence of the Lord." Luke 24:46-47 says, "Then He said to them, 'Thus it is written, and thus it was necessary for the Christ to suffer and to rise from the dead the third day, and that repentance and remission of sins should be preached in His name to all nations, beginning at Jerusalem.'"

In Acts 17:30, we read, "Truly, these times of ignorance God overlooked, but now commands all men everywhere to repent." Further, in Acts 20:20-21, we read of Paul, "how I kept back nothing that was helpful, but proclaimed it to you, and taught you publicly and from house to house, testifying to Jews, and also to Greeks, repentance toward God and faith toward our Lord Jesus Christ."

What is repentance? Repentance simply means to have a change of mind. It comes from the Greek word *Metanoia*. It means that a person has a change of mind. If you were serving one god—an idol in your life—and you decided to forsake that idol and follow Christ, that would be repentance. It's a complete change of direction.

May I ask you a question? Have you repented? I'm not asking if you are a member of a church. Rather, I'm asking if you have turned from your idols and made Jesus Christ the Lord of your life? On the authority of none less than Jesus Christ Himself, I want to share the words of Luke 13:3: "I tell you, no; but unless you repent you will all likewise perish." No repentance; no redemption.

Repentance is a change of mind that leads to a change of life. "No man can serve two masters" (Matthew 6:24). You cannot hold your god of greed with one hand and your God of grace with the other hand. You have to turn from idols to serve the living God. Sadly, many people in our world have never repented of their sins and turned to serve Father God. There has never been a change of mind.

It could be that you want to acquire eternal life just like this rich young ruler did. The Bible never says to accept Jesus as your Savior. Instead, we are told to receive Jesus Christ as our Lord. He is our Savior, but He must also be our Lord. Whatever you trust, if you're not trusting Jesus, you're not going to make it to Heaven.

In today's churches, I think this rich, young ruler would have been happy to accept the feel-good message that's preached. So often, we offer people a little religion, baptism, church membership, and that's it. However, Jesus is not teaching works righteousness. On the contrary, He is teaching that "No man can serve two masters." Jesus' invitation is to come and follow Him wholeheartedly.

WHATEVER MASTER A PERSON CHOOSES WILL MASTER THAT PERSON

Now here's the fourth and final truth I want you to see from this story. Whatever master a person chooses will master that person. In Mark 10:21-22, we read, "One thing you lack: Go your way, sell whatever you have and give to the poor, and you will have treasure in heaven; and come, take up the cross, and follow Me."

In the previous verses, we were discussing repentance. Now, we are talking about faith. The ideas of faith and repentance go hand in hand. When you turn from your sin, you turn to Jesus. This man's sin was greed; he had to turn from it, and he turned to the Lord Jesus Christ. This man needed a new master—Jesus.

How about you? Do you need a new master? Is Jesus Christ the Lord of your life? Romans 10:9-10 tells us, "If you confess with your mouth the Lord Jesus and believe in your heart that God has raised Him from the dead, you will be saved. For with the heart one believes unto righteousness, and with the mouth confession is made unto salvation."

Faith is not merely nodding a head to a series of theological facts about Jesus. It is enthroning Jesus.

In this story, Jesus is giving this man a choice. Obviously, Jesus had struck a vital nerve. Likely this young man began to breathe hard and maybe bite his lip. Possibly, he thought about all of the possessions he had and all that he'd been trusting in for so long. He saw Jesus Christ over here, and he saw eternal life—and there's a choice.

Most likely, the demons of Hell began to whisper to him not to be a fool. At the same time, the Spirit invited him to turn to Christ and find his treasure in heaven. As the perspiration broke out across his forehead, he had to make a choice. And he chose to say no to Jesus and return to his idol. Demons shouted with glee! Angels wept!

Indeed Mark 10:22 is one of the saddest verses in all of the Bible. It reads, "But he was sad at this word, and went away sorrowful, for he had great possessions."

Who knows what this young man might have been to the kingdom of God? He might have been another Timothy. He may have been another apostle Paul. Indeed, he might have been in God's *Who's Who*, but now he's in *Who's Not*. And he's in Hell, and he doesn't have his treasure any longer! Undeniably, he has his false god that will torment him for all eternity. And Jesus let him go. He'll let you go also.

Whatever master a man chooses will master that man. You give your heart to Jesus Christ, and Jesus Christ will master you.

Why is this chapter called, "Three Strikes and You're Out?" I've given it that title because I believe every person has three opportunities to go to Heaven. First, he or she can die before the age of accountability. If you die before the age of accountability (as a young child or a baby) you go straight to Heaven. Heaven is filled with many babies and little children.

Secondly, you have another way by which you can go to heaven. All that is necessary is to be absolutely perfect. Keep the commandments totally. Never sin, anytime or anywhere. But this method is only theoretical because nobody's ever done this, and nobody ever will.

There's one more opportunity for you to go to Heaven and that is to follow Jesus Christ who died upon that cross for you. If you will receive Jesus Christ as your personal Lord and Savior, He will save you. Indeed, He will keep you saved just like He's kept me saved. The Bible says sweetly, plainly, simply, sublimely: "Believe on the Lord Jesus Christ, and you will be saved…" (Acts 16:31).

So, what will you choose today?

ENDNOTES

22. Lyman, D. *The Moral Sayings of Publius Syrus, a Roman Slave*. Cleveland: L. E. Barnard & Company, 1856.

NO OTHER WAY TO HEAVEN EXCEPT THROUGH JESUS

ROMANS 1:16-22

"The burning question is not what God is going to do with the heathen who have never heard, but what is God going to do with those who have heard?"
—*Adrian Rogers*

I s God a righteous God? Is God a just God? Is God fair to let a person die and go to Hell who has never even once heard the name of Jesus? Can those who've never heard of Jesus go to Heaven some other way?

These are good questions, aren't they? God is righteous and God is just. And, there is no other way to Heaven apart from Jesus Christ. Don't get the sentimental idea that all the world religions are somehow connected. They are not. Jesus Christ said in John 14:6, "I am the way, the truth, and the life. No one comes to the Father except through Me."

If somebody can come some other way to heaven, then what does that make Jesus? That makes Jesus a liar. And if Jesus Christ is a liar, He's not my Savior. A liar is nobody's Savior. Consider what Paul said in Acts 4:12: "Nor is there salvation in any other, for there is no other name under heaven given among men by which we must be saved." If Jesus Christ is not the only way, He is none of the ways.

That puts us on the horns of a dilemma, doesn't it? Can a righteous, good, loving, and holy God let a man die and go to hell who never once heard the name of Jesus? That's what today's study in Romans 1 will answer.

Notice how Paul begins in Romans 1:16, "For I am not ashamed of the Gospel of Christ." I've been preaching it now for many years. The more I preach it, the more I marvel in it, the more I thank God for it, the more I stand by it, the more I believe in it.

> For I am not ashamed of the gospel of Christ, for it is the power of God to salvation for everyone who believes, for the Jew first and also for the Greek. For in it the righteousness of God is revealed from faith to faith; as it is written, "The just shall live by faith." For the wrath of God is revealed from heaven against all ungodliness and unrighteousness of men, who suppress the truth in, unrighteousness, because what may be known of God is manifest in them, for God has shown it to them. For since the creation of the world His invisible attributes are clearly seen, being understood by the things that are made, even His eternal power and Godhead, so that they are without excuse. (Romans 1:16-20)

What about those who've never heard the Gospel? If God is just, righteous, and good, why would He let such a thing happen? As we study this passage in Romans today, I want you to notice four factors of faith.

THE REVELATION FACTOR: ALL PEOPLE HAVE SOME LIGHT

Factor number one is the revelation factor. In truth, all people have some light. Imagine, if you will, that the end of time has come. It's that time we know as the *final judgment*. At this final judgment, there will those who've never heard the Gospel of Jesus Christ. The accusation is made; the indictment is given, "For the wrath of God is revealed from heaven against all ungodliness and unrighteousness of men, who suppress the truth in, unrighteousness" (v. 18). The heathens at the judgment could say, "Your Honor, not guilty, not guilty! We never heard the Gospel; we never knew how to be saved. We are innocent by reason of ignorance."

At that time, the Apostle Paul becomes the prosecuting attorney. He says to the Father, "Your Honor, I will prove that they are guilty. I will prove that they are not innocent because of ignorance. I will show that they cannot say they never had a fair and an equal chance. And I call two witnesses to testify against these who say they never knew, they never heard."

Paul will continue, "Witness number one, will you take the stand? Witness number one, give the court your name."

He says, "My name is Creation."

"Oh, Creation, you're the witness that God exists?" asks Paul.

"Yes, I am the witness that God exists."

Then Paul says, "I want you to read Romans 1:19-20, 'because what may be known of God is manifest in them, for God has shown it to them. For since the creation of the world His invisible attributes are clearly seen, being understood by the things that are made, even His eternal power and Godhead, so that they are without excuse.' Now if you have a creation, you have to have a Creator."

When I see a piano here and it's finely tuned, I know that somebody crafted it. When I see a watch that runs with precision most of the time, I know that somebody crafted that watch. When I see a building put together in symmetry and balance and purpose, I know that a talented architect planned and oversaw the construction process.

Similarly, when I see this mighty universe put together, I know that there must be a wise and intelligent Creator. That's the reason the Bible says in Psalm 14:1, "The fool has said in his heart, 'There is no God.'"

Go back with me now to the end-times courtroom and watch Creation step down from the witness stand. The Apostle Paul says,

49

"Now I call my second witness. Would you take the stand? Will you tell the truth, the whole truth and nothing but the truth?"

"I will," says Witness number two.

"Will you give your name?" asks Paul.

Witness number two says, "My name is Conscience."

In the court of faith, there are two witnesses. Number one is Creation; that is the outward, objective witness. The second is Conscience; that is the inward, subjective witness. Romans 1:19 says, "because what may be known of God is manifest in them, for God has shown it to them." Unto them is creation, in them is conscience.

Check out Romans 2:14-15 where we read, "for when Gentiles, who do not have the law, by nature do the things in the law, these, although not having the law, are a law to themselves, who show the work of the law written in their hearts, their conscience also bearing witness, and between themselves their thoughts accusing or else excusing them)."

There is a built-in knowledge of God. All of creation knows internally that there is a Creator. Augustine of Hippo said in his *Confessions* writings, "The soul of man is restless until it rests in God."[23] God made man to serve Him, to know Him, and until he does, he's like a round peg in a square hole, or he is out of fellowship.

So, what is an atheist? There's no real intellectual atheist. They're atheists because of moral problems. But, you may know some brilliant people who are atheists. I know some brilliant people who are not. You may also know some foolish people who believe in God. Yet, it's not a matter of intelligence.

The Bible says in Romans 1:22, "Professing to be wise, they became fools." Why? Because, you see, all of us have a God-consciousness. It is not a matter of intellectualism; it is a matter of morality. "The fool has said in his heart, 'There is no God,'" (Psalm 14:1).

Indeed, an atheist is somebody who has an idea of God, and it makes him uncomfortable. With everything in him, he tries to get rid of his idea of God. However, down deep, none of us can completely dismiss God. Otherwise, we become like a man who bought a new boomerang and killed himself trying to throw the old one away. The idea of God is just there, and the more we try to get rid of it, the more we subconsciously know that God exists.

This first factor is the revelation factor. It is true: all people have some light, some knowledge that there is a God. Consider John 1:9: "That [Christ] was the true Light which gives light to every man coming into the world."

THE REFUSAL FACTOR: LIGHT REFUSED INCREASES DARKNESS

Secondly, there is a refusal factor in the life of faith. And what is this factor? Light refused increases darkness. Look again at Romans 1:21: "Because, although they knew God, they did not glorify Him as God, nor were thankful, but became futile in their thoughts, and their foolish hearts were darkened." Darkened. All men have some light. Light refused increases darkness.

You cannot just simply take light or truth and put it on ice. You cannot put truth in your pocket and choose to pull it out when you need it. When God gives you light, when creation and conscience speak to the heart of any individual anywhere on the face of this earth, we will respond. We cannot remain static. Either we will begin to move toward the Light, or we will regress and lose the light that we have. In time, if we continue to refuse the Light, our hearts will become darkened.

In the Bible, the opposite of truth is not error, it is sin. The error is the baggage that comes with the sin. Why do we refuse truth? We refuses truth because of the sin that is in our hearts. Look at Romans 1:18. "For the wrath of God is revealed from heaven against all ungodliness and unrighteousness of men, who suppress the truth in unrighteousness."

Focus on the word *suppress*. Do you know what that word suppress means? It literally means to resist and smother the truth. And how do they suppress the truth? Not in error, but in unrighteousness.

Why does a man not believe in God? Because the belief in God means that he has to adjust his lifestyle. In his lifestyle, he must give up unrighteousness. Creation and conscience tell him there's a God. Once he recognizes there is a God, he has a decision about how he will live. He will have to choose to live in either the darkness or the light.

One of the most graphic illustrations of this principle is found in the book of 2 Thessalonians 2:9-12. I think these are some of the most terrifying Scriptures in all of the Bible. Speaking of the Antichrist who's coming, it says,

> The coming of the lawless one is according to the working of Satan, with all power, signs, and lying wonders, and with all unrighteous deception among those who perish, because they did not receive the love of the truth, that they might be saved. And for this reason God will send them strong delusion, that they should believe the lie, that they all may be condemned who did not believe the truth but had pleasure in unrighteousness.

Why on earth would God send them strong delusion? Well, just continue to read, "That they should believe a lie." It gets worse, doesn't it? God sends delusion, and why does God send delusion? "That they should believe a lie" (v. 11).

Why would God send a lie? Let's continue to read: "And for this reason God will send them strong delusion, that they should believe the lie, that they all may be condemned." Seems to get worse, doesn't it? Here God sends delusion; they believe a lie that they all might be condemned.

Why? Why would God do that? Well, continue to read in verse 12: "that they all may be condemned who did not believe the truth but had pleasure in unrighteousness." They heard the truth! They knew the truth! However, they turned from the truth! They had pleasure in their filthy, dirty, rotten sin! And God allowed them to stay there.

Let me illustrate it this way. Suppose a man who comes to visit our church on a Sunday when we are taking up a special offering. This man gets offended by the request for money and goes away upset, complaining about churches always wanting money. He vows never to return to church.

Of course, that's not the truth. We talk about so much more than money in our church. But you see, this man's problem is not the truth. He doesn't stop to ask for the truth. In fact, he likely knows that if he'd open the Bible and listen to the Spirit of God that the truth is there. Sadly, his problem is his greed! That's why he got so upset to begin with. So he leaves the church and says, "I am never going back to that church again."

Suppose that he's home on a Sunday morning several months from now. Somebody knocks on the door as he's sitting on his couch reading the paper and drinking a beer. Unshaven and alone, he's at home while his family is at church. As he opens the door, he sees two Jehovah's Witnesses. And he says, "What do you want?"

They say, "We're here to tell you there is no hell."

He says, "Come in. Come in." And he listens to them. They tell him a lie! He believes a lie! He's damned and lost and on the road to the very hell he says he doesn't believe in!

Why? He wouldn't receive the love of the truth. Instead, he chose to have pleasure in unrighteousness. This is what the scripture is talking about when it ways, "And for this reason God will send them strong delusion, that they should believe the lie, that they all may be condemned who did not believe the truth but had pleasure in unrighteousness" (2 Thessalonians 2:11-12).

All people have some light. That's the revelation factor. The refusal factor is light refused increases darkness. You don't just put truth on ice. Mark 4:25 tells us, "For whoever has, to him more will be given; but whoever does not have, even what he has will be taken away from him."

THE RECEPTION FACTOR: LIGHT OBEYED INCREASES LIGHT

Now, here's the third factor I'd like to invite you consider. Go back to Romans 1:22: "Professing themselves to be wise, they became fools." They are the ones who think we're the fools. Now they may be a Ph.D., but in spiritual things it stands for *phenomenal dud*. They worship science as a god rather than worshipping the God of science. They never ask how creation came about in the first place.

This third principle of faith is the reception factor. All people have some light; that's the revelation factor. The refusal factor is light refused increases darkness; their foolish heart was darkened. The reception factor is this: light obeyed increases light.

Creation and conscience only bring us to the fact of God. But you see that if a man is not interested in the FACT of God, he's certainly not going to be interested in the WAY to God. And God is under no obligation to show any man the WAY to God who's not even interested in the FACT of God. When men or women become vain in their imagination, they will have their hearts darkened. But, when they are receptive to the Light, they will have light increasing!

Look if you will again in Romans 1:16: "For I am not ashamed of the gospel of Christ, for it is the power of God to salvation for everyone who believes, for the Jew first and also for the Greek. For in it the righteousness of God is revealed from faith to faith." Now here's the righteousness of God. Is God righteous? Yes! And how is the righteousness of God revealed? "From faith to faith." That's the revelation factor. God gives you truth; you believe that truth. Then, God gives you more truth. The more you obey the light, the more light you get.

When a person seeks to know more of God, then God gives him more light and more understanding. That's faith. A seeker of the true Light will go from faith to faith. When a person is ready to receive the Gospel, God will get the Gospel to that person if He has to wreck an airplane and parachute a missionary to do it.

I believe with all of my heart there's never been a man or woman who ever lived on the face of this earth who died without some opportunity to have received Christ if they were open to the light that God gave them. While all men don't have enough light to save them, all men have enough light to damn them. Had they lived up to the light that they had, they would have received more light, and, according to Romans 1:17, "For in it the righteousness of God is from faith to faith."

There are numerous illustrations of this principle in the Bible. Consider the Ethiopian eunuch in Acts 8. This man had been to Jerusalem, the most religious city on the face of the earth. Why had he gone there? He had gone there to worship. He'd come all the way in a chariot from northern Africa, from Ethiopia, in that day when there were no airplanes.

While in Jerusalem—the most religious city on the face of the earth—he was seeking God. But the wells of religion in Jerusalem were dry. As he is traveling home and reading the book of Isaiah, he's trying to understand what he is reading.

It is in this moment that God called a preacher named Phillip to leave a revival service in Samaria and go to this man. Philip obediently went and shared with this many about Jesus. The Ethiopian eunuch, that opportunity on wheels, got saved. He was searching for light, and God gave him more light. (See Acts 8:26-39.)

Another great example of light is the story of Cornelius found in Acts 10. The Bible tells us that Cornelius was a Gentile; he was not of the household of Israel. But Cornelius, an army officer, had a hunger to know God. I don't know where he got that hunger. Perhaps he looked into the starry heavens one night while he was on patrol duty and wondered Who created it all.

In response to Cornelius' searching, God sent Peter to talk to him about Jesus. Peter shared with him how he could be saved, and he was. The principle is clear: when you obey the light that you have, God will give you even more light.

Sadly, the reason that some of us don't understand the Bible any more than we do is that we have not been living up to the light that God has already giving us. Why should God show you more in the Word of God until you obey what you already know? Isn't that a good question?

You ask for more revelation and wisdom, but you aren't obeying what God has already shown you. Matthew 25:29 says, "For to everyone who has, more will be given, and he will have abundance; but from him who does not have, even what he has will be taken away."

The principle is clear: light obeyed increases light! And if you want to understand the part of the Bible you don't understand, begin to obey the part you do understand, and you'll understand what you didn't understand! Do you understand?

In summary, obey what God teaches you. The problem is not in the head; the problem is in the heart. One of the greatest promises in all of the Bible is in John 7. The people were wondering about Jesus Christ. The Pharisees were testing Him, taunting Him, and picking at Him. And, Jesus threw out this challenge, one of the greatest challenges in all of the Bible.

Jesus said in John 7:17, "If anyone wills to do His will, he shall know concerning the doctrine, whether it is from God or whether I speak on My own authority." Whether Jesus was a megalomaniac, some peasant prophet who has a messianic complex, or whether He came from God, He told them to do the will of God, and then they would know the truth.

When I was in the Space Center down at Merritt Island, I was in my office one day and a man drove up in a Cadillac. After parking his car, he came into my office and told me he wanted to talk to me. He was one of the executives at the Space Center, helping to put a man on the moon.

I said to him, "Well, what do you want to talk about?"

He said, "I want to talk about my wife. She wants to commit suicide and I don't want her to. Would you talk with my wife?"

I said, "Well, I will if you'll come with her."

So the two of them came and sat down and I said, "Tell me, lady, what your problems are." And her problems were this man! This man was a liar, a drunk, an adulterer, a gambler, and a wife abuser. He was a rotten person.

In learning this, I just stopped talking to her and I started talking to him. I said, "Sir, I want to ask you a question. Are you a Christian?"

He laughed a scornful laugh and said, "No! I'm not a Christian; I'm an atheist."

I said, "Oh, an atheist." I said, "An atheist is a man who says there's no God, and he knows there's no God. Do you know there's no God?"

He said, "Yes."

I said, "Well that's interesting." I said, "Of all there is to know, how much do you know? Would you, do you know half of everything there is to know?"

He said, "Of course not."

I shot back, "But you said you know there's no God. Wouldn't you have to admit the possibility that God might exist in that half of the knowledge you don't have?"

Well, he said, "I...OK," said, "You got me, I'm not an atheist; I'm an agnostic."

I said, "Well," I said, "That's just a fancy word for a doubter. Are you a doubter?"

He said, "Yes, and a big one."

I said, "I don't care what size, I want to know what kind."

He said, "What do you mean?"

I said, "Well, there're two kinds of doubters. There are honest doubters and dishonest doubters. Which kind are you?"

He said, "Well what's the difference?"

I said, "An honest doubter doesn't know, but he wants to know, and therefore he investigates. A dishonest doubter doesn't know because he doesn't want to know, and he can't find God for the same reason a thief can't find a policeman. In fact, Jesus said in John 3:20, 'For everyone practicing evil hates the light and does not come to the light, lest his deeds should be exposed.'"

He said, "Well."

I said, "Sir, would you like to find out whether you're an honest doubter or a dishonest doubter?"

He said, "Yes."

I said, "Would you sign this statement: God, I don't know whether You exist or not. I don't know whether the Bible is Your Word or not. I don't know whether Jesus Christ is Your Son or not. I don't know, but I want to know. And because I want to know, I will make an honest investigation. And because it is an honest investigation, I will follow the results of that investigation wherever they lead me, regardless of the cost."

I said, "Would you sign that statement?"

He said, "Give it to me again."

I repeated myself, "God, I don't know whether You exist or not. I don't know whether the Bible is Your Word or not. I don't know whether Jesus Christ is Your Son or not, but I want to know and because I want to know, I'll make an honest investigation. And because it is an honest investigation, I will follow the results of that investigation wherever they lead me, regardless of the cost."

He said, "I'd like to be honest."

I said, "Wonderful!" Then, I gave him an assignment. I said, "I want you to begin to read the Gospel of John, because," I said, "the purpose of that book is written that you might believe that Jesus is the Christ and believing, that you might have life through His name."

He said, "But I don't believe."

I said, "That's all right. You just make an honest investigation. You say to God, 'God I don't know whether this is Your Word or not. If this is Your Word, show me, and I make up my mind before the fact that I will obey You only if You show me this is Your Word and speak to my heart.'"

He said, "That's fair enough."

A few weeks later, he came back to my office and said, "I believe that Jesus Christ is the Son of God." He got on his knees like a little child and wept his way to the arms of Jesus. That was many, many years ago.

Not too long ago, I got a letter from this man. He lives in Bangor, Maine now. And, would you believe that he has a ministry teaching the Bible? His words to me in the letter read, "Mr. Rogers, I want to thank you for spending time with this general in the devil's army."

Where was that man's problem? He thought his problem was intellectual. However, his problem wasn't intellectual; his problem was his will. When a man surrenders his will to God, God will speak to him. Light obeyed increases light! Live up to the light that you have, and God will give you more light.

THE RECKONING FACTOR: GOD WILL JUDGE US BY THE LIGHT WE'VE REJECTED

Finally, there is one more factor of faith. Factor number one is the revelation factor. Factor number two is the refusal factor. Factor number three is the reception factor. Factor number four is the reckoning factor.

When God comes to judge us, what is God going to judge us by? Do you think that God is going to judge us by the sin we have committed? No! God is going to judge us by the light we've rejected. God is going to judge us by the light we have rejected! I want you to see this; it's very clear in the Word of God. Look in Romans 2:5:

"But in accordance with your hardness and your impenitent heart you are treasuring up for yourself wrath in the day of wrath and revelation of the righteous judgment of God."

Now read with me Romans 2:11-12, "For there is no partiality with God. For as many as have sinned without law will also perish without law, and as many as have sinned in the law will be judged by the law." What does this mean? Paul is simply saying this: that God knows how much light you have.

Many of us have far more light than other people have, not because you necessarily sought it. Many of you live where there's a church on every street corner. There are Bibles available everywhere you look. By the providence of God you have more light than others have.

In the judgment, God is going to hold you accountable more so than the person who's never heard the Gospel. Consider the words of Luke 12:48: "But he who did not know, yet committed things deserving of stripes, shall be beaten with few. For everyone to whom much is given, from him much will be required; and to whom much has been committed, of him they will ask the more."

Truly, it would be horrible for the pagan in darkest Africa to die and go to hell. How sad that a person never heard the name of Jesus and refused to live up to the light that he did have. But how much more tragic it would be for a person who has easy access to the Gospel to refuse it and go to hell.

The burning question is not what is God going to do with the heathen who never heard. The burning question is what is God going to do with you, who heard the Gospel of Jesus. If you have heard the message that Jesus died in agony and blood upon the cross, and you said, "No!" to the Lord Jesus, this is most grievous decision of all.

Don't ever say you didn't have a chance. And Jesus said to Capernaum in Matthew 10:15, His headquarter city, "it will be more tolerable for the land of Sodom and Gomorrah in the day of judgment, than for that city." This is where He preached and taught and yet they turned their back on Him and never received Him.

All men have some light. Light refused increases darkness. Light obeyed increases light. And men are judged according to the light that they have. God is righteous. "For I am not ashamed of the gospel of Christ, for it is the power of God to salvation for everyone who believes" (Romans 1:16).

And I promise you on the authority of the Word of God, if you believe in Jesus today, He'll save you, because He saved me. Won't you invite Him to save you today?

ENDNOTES

23.   Anderson, Suzanne. "Walking Our Faith: 'Our Heart Is Restless until It Rests in You'." *SummitDaily.com*, SummitDaily.com, 4 Mar. 2017, www.summitdaily.com/news/walking-our-faith-our-heart-is-restless-until-it-rests-in-you/.

WHAT SHALL I DO WITH JESUS?

MATTHEW 27:22

"Nobody can stay neutral. You will have to do something with our Lord and Savior, Jesus Christ."
—*Adrian Rogers*

What is the greatest question that has ever been asked? Do you recall that Pontius Pilate was the Governor of Judea at the time Jesus was judged worthy of death and sentenced to die upon a cross? When Pilate had Jesus before him, he had to make a decision concerning the Lord Jesus Christ. He asked a question that we find in Matthew 27:22: "What then shall I do with Jesus who is called Christ?" I submit to you that no greater question could be asked than this one.

At this juncture in history, Jesus was before Pilate with His future hanging in the balance. Indeed, there's coming a day when Pilate will stand before Jesus to be judged by Jesus. But, in this moment, Pilate had Jesus' future in his hands.

What does that have to do with all of us? Well, in a very real sense, Pilate represents every man, woman, boy, and girl upon the face of the earth who's asked the same question, "What then shall I do with Jesus who is called Christ?"

As Jesus was before Pilate, Jesus is also before you. As Jesus was in Pilate's hands, Jesus is in your hands. And, just as Pilate will stand before Jesus, so will you and I will also stand before Jesus. I ask you today to answer that same question: what will you do with Jesus? Your answer to this question is so important.

First of all, this question matters because it is a present question. You are going to answer that question today. What will you do? And it is not only a present question, it is also a personal question. Personally, you're going to decide what you're going to do with the Lord Jesus Christ.

In addition, it's a very pertinent question. Your destiny hangs on your answer to this question of what you do with the Lord Jesus Christ. Finally, it is a pressing question. You will answer—one way or another. Even if you don't want to answer this question. It is inescapable, and unavoidable. Will you accept Him or reject Him? Will you confess Him or deny Him? Will you crown Him or crucify Him? Nobody can stay neutral. You will have to do something with our Lord and Savior, Jesus Christ.

In this chapter, I want us to take a look at Pilate's decision. I want us to see the tragic decision that Pilate made. And, I pray we will make a better decision than he did. Let's look closely at this story in Matthew 27.

THE VOICES THAT CONFRONTED PILATE

First of all, Pilate has Jesus in front of him. Jesus is the unavoidable, inescapable, inevitable fact of life. And I want you to notice the many voices that confronted Pilate on that day. To begin with, there was what I want to call the voice of reason. The Bible says of Pilate, "For he knew that they had handed Him over because of envy" (Matthew 27:18).

As Pilate read the hearts and minds of those who brought Jesus before him, he heard them crying out for the blood of Jesus.

These religious leaders wanted Jesus crucified. But Pilate was no fool. You don't get to be the Governor of Judea under the Romans by being a fool. He knew men. And he knew what the scriptures tell us, "that they had handed Him over because of envy." Truly, Pilate knew that the charges were trumped up against Jesus.

This voice of reason spoke to Pilate. He knew better when he allowed Jesus Christ to be crucified. In like manner, the voice of reason is speaking to you. If you will be reasonable, if you will do what Pilate did, examine the evidence and listen to the witnesses, you will have to say that Jesus Christ is the Son of God, worthy of all honor, glory, majesty, and praise. For a person to crucify Jesus, he must also crucify reason.

C. S. Lewis taught us the principle that Jesus Christ is one of three persons. It is called a *trilemma*. In this trilemma, Lewis maintained that Jesus was either *"Lunatic, Liar, or Lord."* Put another way, Jesus was either, *"Mad, Bad, or God."*[24] Do you believe that Jesus Christ was—is—a liar? Or else, if He was not a liar, was He a lunatic? Some mad man who thought He was God, but wasn't? Deranged, guilty of megalomania? Or, was He the Lord?

Was He who He said He was and claimed to be? Those are your three choices. Choose one: Lunatic, Liar, or Lord. What does reason tell you? The voice of reason confronted Pilate, and the voice of reason confronts you and me as well.

Equally important, there's another voice that confronted Pilate, and it was the voice of a loved one. Look in Matthew 27:19: "While he was sitting on the judgment seat, his wife sent to him, saying, 'Have nothing to do with that just Man, for I have suffered many things today in a dream because of Him.'"

It seems that Pilate's wife was somehow in contact with God. God had spoken to her and she went to warn Pilate. Have you ever had a family member speak to you about Jesus? Perhaps a father, a mother, a brother, or a sister? Maybe someone has pled with you to do the right thing concerning Jesus Christ?

Equally important, the voice of his own conscience confronted him that day. Pilate's conscience thundered within him. He knew that Jesus was innocent. Look in Matthew 27:22-23: "Pilate said to them, 'What then shall I do with Jesus who is called Christ?'

They all said to him, 'Let Him be crucified!' Then the governor said, 'Why, what evil has He done?' But they cried out all the more, saying, 'Let Him be crucified!'"

In his conscience, Pilate must have known what he was doing was wrong. Of course, these decisions must have made him feel dirty, grimy, and somehow soiled by this whole mock trial. And, today, it could be that you feel the same way. You've never given your heart to Jesus although reason says that you should. Loved ones say that you should. And your own conscience reverberates in your soul to tell you that you need to do the right thing with the Lord Jesus.

Additionally, there was a fourth voice that spoke to Pilate. It was the voice of Jesus Christ Himself. Jesus spoke to Pilate. In John 18:37, we read, "Pilate therefore said to Him, 'Are You a king then?' Jesus answered, 'You say rightly that I am a king. For this cause I was born, and for this cause I have come into the world, that I should bear witness to the truth. Everyone who is of the truth hears My voice.'" Clearly, Pilate heard the voice of Jesus.

It could be that you have also heard all of these voices. You have heard the voice of reason, the voice of a loved one, and the voice of your own conscience. However, you don't believe you've ever heard the voice of Jesus. It's important to note that every time you read or hear the words of the Bible, you are hearing the voice of Jesus. That's how God speaks—through the pages of scripture. Are you listening?

THE VALUES THAT CONFORMED PILATE

Not only were there voices that confronted Pilate, there were also values that conformed him. Certainly, there were pressures on Pilate that warred against him making the right decision. What were some of these pressures?

First, there was the pressure of public opinion. Look at Matthew 27:20: "But the chief priests and elders persuaded the multitudes that they should ask for Barabbas and destroy Jesus." During this trial, there was a multitude, a large crowd that was clamoring for the criminal Barabbas to be released. At the same time, they were calling for Jesus to be crucified. Poor Pilate was a politician. He was reading the polls, and he wanted to do what the crowds wanted.

Further evidence of this public pressure on Pilate is found in Mark 15:15. It reads, "And so Pilate, willing to content the people, released Barabbas unto them, and delivered Jesus, when he had scourged Him, to be crucified" (KJV). Think about that phrase, "Willing to gratify the crowd." Public opinion persuaded Pilate and impacted his decision.

Did you know that public opinion also impacts us and the decisions we make for Christ today? What people think and what people say affects us? Being politically correct is huge in our day. We're so concerned about public opinion and wanting to please the crowd that sometimes we crucify Jesus in order to please the crowd.

A second factor that conformed Pilate's decision was the matter of his pride. Pilate was a very proud man. In John 19:9, we read another conversation between Jesus and Pilate. Speaking of Pilate, the scripture says, "and went again into the Praetorium, and said to Jesus, 'Where are You from?' But Jesus gave him no answer."

Pilate continues in verse 10, "'Are You not speaking to me? Do You not know that I have power to crucify You, and power to release You?'" Do you hear the pride? It's very obvious that Pilate is an egotist, quite full of himself.

In response, "Jesus answered, 'You could have no power at all against Me unless it had been given you from above. Therefore the one who delivered Me to you has the greater sin'" (v. 11). Jesus told Pilate that he had no power over Him. Only God had the power.

So, what was it that was squeezing Pilate? First, there was public pressure. Second, there was his pride squeezing and molding him. And, finally, there was the pressure of his position and his possessions. For you see, Pilate had a cushy job. He was the Governor and he could do whatever he liked. However, in this case, if Pilate did not make the politically correct decision, he could lose his job.

Consider the words of John 19:12: "From then on Pilate sought to release Him, but the Jews cried out, saying, 'If you let this Man go, you are not Caesar's friend. Whoever makes himself a king speaks against Caesar.'" In other words, the crowd was pressuring him with Caesar's displeasure and the potential loss of his job.

It's possible that you may be afraid to give your heart to Jesus because you are worried about what it may cost you. It may be that you could lose your job, or a promotion, or a pay raise if you become a Christian. Indeed, you may feel pressures that keep you from a relationship with Jesus because of what you fear you could lose. Pilate was afraid of what he might lose. Are you?

THE VERDICT THAT CONDEMNED PILATE

There's one final factor in Pilate's decision. It's the verdict that condemned him. We see this verdict from the crowd in Matthew 27:26: "Then he released Barabbas to them; and when he had scourged Jesus, he delivered Him to be crucified." Pilate delivered Jesus to be crucified. Why did he do this? We know there was pressure upon him. And, he waffled quite a bit during these proceedings.

First of all, he simply tried to ignore Jesus—as if he could somehow put Him off or put Him away. In John 18:31, we read, "Then Pilate said to them, 'You take Him and judge Him according to your law.' Therefore the Jews said to him, 'It is not lawful for us to put anyone to death.'" The people brought Jesus to Pilate asking for Him to be put to death. Pilate refused and told them to judge Jesus by their Jewish laws. He challenged them to deal with Him and tried to ignore Jesus somehow.

By the same token, people try to ignore Jesus today. They think He is for everyone else and don't want to be bothered with Him. They'd just rather not deal with Jesus right now. However, ignoring Jesus doesn't ultimately provide a solution. Either we will decide what to do with Jesus now, or we will face Him one day at the judgment.

Secondly, Pilate tried to shift the decision to someone else. When he heard that Jesus was from Galilee, he tried to shift the ruling to King Herod's court. In Luke 23:6-7, we read, "When Pilate heard of Galilee, he asked if the Man were a Galilean. And as soon as he knew that He belonged to Herod's jurisdiction, he sent Him to Herod, who was also in Jerusalem at that time."

May I tell you something? Sin is personal, and so is your decision, and nobody can make the decision for Christ for you. Your parents, your rabbi, your priest, a politician—none of these people can make the decision for you. You cannot shift the decision to somebody else. You have a decision to make. What will you do with Jesus?

When Pilate sent Jesus to Herod, Herod send him right back. Herod didn't want to deal with Jesus. We read in Luke 23:8-11 this part of the story:

> Now when Herod saw Jesus, he was exceedingly glad; for he had desired for a long time to see Him, because he had heard many things about Him, and he hoped to see some miracle done by Him. Then he questioned Him with many words, but He answered him nothing. And the chief priests and scribes stood and vehemently accused Him. Then Herod, with his men of war, treated Him with contempt and mocked Him, arrayed Him in a gorgeous robe, and sent Him back to Pilate.

Next, after trying to shift the decision to Herod, Pilate tried something else. He tried to admire Jesus. He thought if he could give some platitudes about Jesus, if he could say some nice things about Jesus, then perhaps it would be all right. In Luke 23:13-15, we read,

> Then Pilate, when he had called together the chief priests, the rulers, and the people, said to them, "You have brought this Man to me, as one who misleads the people. And indeed, having examined Him in your presence, I have found no fault in this Man concerning those things of which you accuse Him; no, neither did Herod, for I sent you back to him; and indeed nothing deserving of death has been done by Him."

Think about it. Pilate, who allowed Jesus to be crucified, who by his own words could have released Jesus or crucified Jesus, said this, "I have found no fault in this Man." And yet, he allowed Him to be crucified. Do you know what he was doing? Pilate thought that if he just said some nice words about Jesus, it would make everything okay.

Truthfully, it would been better for Pilate to have found fault in Jesus. Of course, there was none. But it would have been better for him to have fault in Jesus, or even to have thought that he found fault in Jesus, than to find no fault in Him and allow Him to be crucified. It would have been better for him to have been a pagan who'd never heard of Jesus than to say, "I have found no fault in this Man," and then simply admire Him and then allow Him to be crucified.

Interestingly, many people still try this trick today. Many try to say nice things about Jesus. However, it is not enough for you to tip the hat to Jesus; you must bow the knee to Jesus. It is not enough for you just to say, "I have found no fault in this Man," and think, therefore, that you are all right. Instead, you must acknowledge Him as your Lord and Savior. That is the only way.

Pilate did one final thing that condemned him. Ineffectively, he attempted to remain neutral. He thought that he could just simply wash his hands of the whole matter. Notice the story in Luke 23:22-24,

> Then he said to them the third time, "Why, what evil has He done? I have found no reason for death in Him. I will therefore chastise Him and let Him go." But they were insistent, demanding with loud voices that He be crucified. And the voices of these men and of the chief priests prevailed. So Pilate gave sentence that it should be as they requested.

In essence, Pilate gave them what they wanted and then tried to wash his hands of the whole affair. He tried to remain neutral and act as if he played no part in the situation. But, trying not to decide is ultimately to decide. That's why Jesus said in Matthew 12:30, "He who is not with Me is against Me, and he who does not gather with Me scatters abroad."

That being the case, an ocean full of water could not have washed the sin from Pilate's hands. And when the gavel fell in Pilate's court, there was another gavel that fell in Heaven. When Pilate allowed Jesus to be condemned, Pilate himself was condemned. With this in mind, you cannot be neutral concerning the Lord Jesus Christ.

CONCLUSION

The first trial of the Lord Jesus was a mockery of justice. So, I'm going to put Jesus on trial again today. Imagine, if you will, that Jesus is on the stand today. You are the jury, and I ask that you make a decision about His fate. I'll bring several witnesses to testify and share truth with this mock court. In the end, you will have to determine what to do with Jesus.

To begin with, I call John the Baptist to the stand. Of John the Baptist, Matthew 11:11 tells us, "Assuredly, I say to you, among those born of women there has not risen one greater than John the Baptist; but he who is least in the kingdom of heaven is greater than he."

"Now, John, you baptized Jesus in the River Jordan. You knew Jesus from boyhood. John, would you tell the court and tell the jury what think you of Christ?"

Hear John the Baptist as he says, "Behold! The Lamb of God who takes away the sin of the world!" (John 1:29).

"Thank you, John, for that testimony. You may be seated."

Next, I'd like to call another who often spoke, sometimes thoughtlessly, to the stand. "Simon Peter, will you take the stand and tell us what you think of Jesus?"

Simon Peter says to Jesus, "You are the Christ, the Son of the living God" (Matthew 16:16).

And now I'm going to call a sort of a mystic, a man who has a pensive and thoughtful spirit, different perhaps from Peter. I call John the apostle. "John, you were with the Lord Jesus. Would you tell us what you think of Him?"

Hear the Apostle John as he says, "And the Word became flesh and dwelt among us, and we beheld His glory, the glory as of the only begotten of the Father, full of grace and truth" (John 1:14).

Next, I call Thomas to the stand. "Thomas, you were a follower of His. For a while you had difficulty believing. Thomas, you saw the nail prints in His hands and in His side. Thomas, would you tell the court and tell the jury what you think of Christ?"

Thomas bows his knee and he says, "My Lord and my God!" (John 20:28).

Is there a woman who can testify? "Martha, would you come, tell the truth, the whole truth, and nothing but the truth? This man spent many happy days in your home. You've observed Him in all sorts of situations. Martha, would you tell the courtroom what you think of Him?"

Martha says, "Lord, I believe that You are the Christ, the Son of God" (John 11:27).

Well, but these are all humans. Is there some other being that we might call? Could we summon an angel? Put an angel under oath? "Angel, would you tell us who this man Jesus is?"

See the angel as he stands and looks into the face of Jesus and says, "For there is born to you this day in the city of David a Savior, who is Christ the Lord" (Luke 2:11).

What about some of Jesus' enemies? Let's hear from one of the Pharisees who wanted Him crucified. "Pharisee, wrap your self-righteous robes around you and look at Jesus, and tell us why you wanted Him crucified."

The Pharisee answers, "This Man receives sinners and eats with them" (Luke 15:2).

Next, let's call Caiaphas, the high priest, to testify. "Caiaphas, you were the high priest who wanted Him crucified. Caiaphas, you tell us why you wanted Jesus crucified?"

Caiaphas answers, "He said He is the Son of God" (Matthew 26:57-66).

Now, I'd like to call the centurion to testify. "You helped drive those scalding nails into His quivering palms. Centurion, tell us now. You watched Him die."

The centurion says, "Truly this Man was the Son of God" (Mark 15:39).

Additionally, let's call Judas to the stand. "You betrayed Him and sold Him for thirty pieces of silver. Judas, would you tell us what you think of Him?"

Judas says, "I have sinned by betraying innocent blood" (Matthew 27:4).

Let's have Pilate come to the stand. "Pilate! You had Him crucified. Tell us what you think of Him."

Pilate says, "I find no fault in Him" (John 19:4).

I've called angels. Why not a demon? All right, I summon a filthy, dirty demon from the pit. "Demon, I adjure you by God, tell the truth."

The demon answers, "I know who You are—the Holy One of God" (Luke 4:34).

Now, are there any contemporary witnesses? I'm going to ask some of them to share a testimony and tell us what they think of Jesus.

The first contemporary witness steps forward to testify,

My name is Paul Kuhlman, and I was saved January 2, 1977; I was 38 years old. At the time, I was drinking my life away; sober days were few and far between. One night I went to a church service, and I recognized my need for the Lord Jesus Christ. But during the invitation I did not go forward because of pride and embarrassment. When we got home that night, my wife and family went to bed, and I was in my family room by myself. I got down on my knees and I prayed a very simple prayer, "Lord Jesus, please save me." And He did.

The Bible says in 2 Corinthians 5:17, "Therefore, if anyone is in Christ, he is a new creation; old things have passed away; behold, all things have become new." And the first thing that Jesus did was to take away bad habits—the drinking, the smoking, the filthy magazines, and the bad language that I used. The Lord Jesus gave me a new appearance. And He put a new countenance on my face and a new spring in my step. After I met Jesus, He gave me new friends, a new marriage in Christ, a new relationship with all of my children, and a new destiny. I'm on my way to Heaven, and I'm going to be there with the Lord Jesus Christ for eternity.

A second contemporary witness would like to give testimony:

My name is Steven Holly, and this is my wife, Lee. When we first married, I felt like having her as a wife would be the answer to the void that was in my heart. It didn't take long to realize that when you put the burden of your total happiness on an individual, like your spouse, it wears down very quickly.

In a very short time, our marriage began to fall apart. This left an even bigger void in my life. When we became separated, the ache became even greater. At this time, I sought counsel from a man who pointed me to the one true counselor, Jesus. Daily, I began to trust Jesus, seeking Him in prayer and through His Word. I began to realize that I was not alone.

Soon I sought forgiveness of my wife and of God. At the time, my wife was not ready to reconcile, and our marriage sadly ended in divorce. But, Jesus worked in my life and in hers, and after a full year, He brought us back together. Then, He honored us with four wonderful little boys. Our marriage, our life, and our family is a testimony to the fact that if you are hurting or in need, Jesus is your counselor and your healer, and He will comfort you.

And, a final contemporary witness would like to testify:

My name is Debbie Gleason. And there are not adequate words to express the incredible, never-ending and ever-faithful Jesus Christ and what He means to me. Six years ago, my husband, Joe, was diagnosed with colon cancer. Joe's incredibly strong faith and never-wavering belief that God is in total control, kept us focused on eternal things. Throughout his four-year illness, I never once saw him distraught or hopeless because he knew that Heaven was just ahead.

I cannot say that it has been easy; it hasn't. I cannot say that I understand why it happened; I don't. And I can't say that there's not sadness in my heart, for there is. But there is one wonderful lesson I have learned through all this, and that is that no one or nothing can take away my joy, for its foundation is Jesus Christ.

I think back over the last weeks of my husband's life, and he kept saying, "I just don't think God is through with my life yet." And now I know what God was revealing to Joe. He wasn't through; He still isn't through with Joe's life, for I know many, many times I have been strengthened by the way that Joe led his life and the way that God's faithfulness saw us through Joe's death. One of my favorite verses has become 2 Corinthians 4:17. It says, "For our light affliction, which is but for a moment, is working for us a far more exceeding and eternal weight in glory." I know that my Jesus is faithful, for Heaven is still ahead.

I'd like to call one final witness to the stand. With great humility, I call to the witness stand Almighty God. "God the Father, would You tell us, who is Jesus?"

I believe God would repeat the words of Matthew 3:17, "This is My beloved Son, in whom I am well pleased."

Moreover, let me tell you what God the Father did. When they nailed Jesus up on that cross, put Him in the grave, and shouted, "He is worthy of death! Crucify Him," Almighty God reversed the decision of the court and raised Him from the dead. Romans 1:4 tells us, "[Jesus] declared to be the Son of God with power according to the Spirit of holiness, by the resurrection from the dead."

Do I believe that God raised Jesus Christ? Yes, I believe it. The early apostles believed it. Many of them died for their faith. Truly, men may live for a lie, but few men will die for a lie. For the most part, people tell lies to get them out of trouble, not into trouble. But these early Christians were totally convinced that Jesus came out of that grave.

Now, my court case has been presented. You are the jury, and you are going to have the chance to register your decision. What will your decision be with Christ?

Here are your choices:

- You may crown Him or crucify Him.
- You may acknowledge Him or reject Him.
- You may receive Him or deny Him.

However, you have to make a decision; you can't wash your hands or be neutral. To decide not to decide would be the worst decision you could make.

ENDNOTES

24. "Lewis's Trilemma." *Wikipedia*, Wikimedia Foundation, 29 Jan. 2020, en.wikipedia.org/wiki/Lewis%27s_trilemma.

HOW TO BE A
GROWING CHRISTIAN

1 JOHN 2:12-14

"So, what is spiritual maturity? In a just a simple sentence—maturity is Christlikeness."
—Adrian Rogers

L et me ask you a question. Are you a growing Christian? Do you love and know the Lord Jesus Christ better than you did last year or last week? Oliver Cromwell once said, "He who ceases to be better, ceases to be good."[25]

Some Christians are saved, but they're not growing. They are not like a tree; they are like a stump in the ground not growing at all. In fact, you ought to be a growing Christian. You will never know the kind of victory that you ought to know and the kind of joy that you may have unless you learn to be a growing Christian. To grow as a Christian is to mature. You can be young only once, but you can be immature for a long time. You can be 40 or 50 years old, and still be spiritually immature.

Consider what the Bible says in Hebrews 6:1 where it tells us that we are to go on toward maturity. The Amplified Bible translates in this way: "advancing steadily toward the completeness and perfection that belong to spiritual maturity." That's God's plan for all believers—that we advance steadily toward spiritual maturity.

With this in mind, I want to talk to you about how you can continue to grow and mature as a Christian. First of all, let's consider what maturity is spiritually and what it is not. You can be spiritually healthy and not mature. A five-year-old child can be healthier than a 50-year old man, but he is not mature.

You may be a new Christian, and you're rejoicing in the Lord Jesus Christ. Indeed, you are healthy. But that does not mean that you do not need to move forward and mature. You can be gifted and not mature. As a matter of fact, if you're gifted and not mature, you may get yourself and others in a mess. To the Corinthian church, Paul's most carnal church, he said, "so that you come short in no gift, eagerly waiting for the revelation of our Lord Jesus Christ" (1 Corinthians 1:7). They were gifted, but they were not mature. Are you gifted spiritually or are you gifted with talents? You may be, but that doesn't mean that you are mature.

So, what is spiritual maturity? In just a simple sentence— maturity is Christlikeness. Maturity is being like Jesus. The apostle Paul said in Ephesians 4:13, "till we all come to the unity of the faith and the knowledge of the Son of God, to a perfect man, to the measure of the stature of the fullness of Christ." To be perfect doesn't mean that we will become sinless; it means that we will become mature.

In essence, Paul is saying that the goal of his ministry is to present every man a mature Christian. That's the goal of my ministry as well. I thank God for our church buildings, for the Sunday school attendance, for the budget, and for the organization. However, all of that is worth nothing unless you are growing in the grace of our Lord and Savior Jesus Christ.

What is the goal of my ministry, and what is the measurement of my ministry? Very simple: are those in this ministry becoming more like the Lord Jesus Christ? Indeed, if you are becoming more like the Lord Jesus Christ, that is a blessing to me. My prayer is that you might become more like the Lord Jesus Christ.

THE MARKS OF MATURITY

Maturity is a life-long process. To gain maturity, we go through three major stages. Look at 1 John 2:12-14, and let's consider the stages we will grow through as we seek to become more like Jesus.

> I write to you, little children, because your sins are forgiven you for His name's sake. I write to you, fathers, because you have known Him who is from the beginning. I write to you, young men, because you have overcome the wicked one. I write to you, little children, because you have known the Father. I have written to you, fathers, because you have known Him who is from the beginning. I have written to you, young men, because you are strong, and the word of God abides in you, and you have overcome the wicked one.

In these verses, the Apostle John speaks of childhood and little children. Then, he speaks of young manhood. Finally, he speaks of fatherhood. All of us are in one of those three categories: childhood, youth, or parenthood. God loves them all, and God loves you, but God wants to move you in progression through these stages until you come to the parenthood stage. In our physical lives, we are babies, children, youth, adults, and then we grow up and become fathers and mothers.

The Thrilling Wonders of Childhood

What is the mark of a childlike Christian? Little children know the thrilling wonders of childhood. In 1 John 2:12, John says, "I write to you, little children, because your sins are forgiven you for His name's sake."

When a person becomes a newborn babe in Christ, what is the mark? Well, he or she is thrilled at knowing Jesus. There is great joy in forgiven sins that are buried in the grave of God's forgetfulness. There is such joy in coming into a relationship with Jesus.

Typically, little children live in the realm of their feelings. Everything is exciting and full of wonder. Maybe you're like a little child right now spiritually. Possibly you've been saved in the last year, and you just can't get over it. Everything is exciting, joy-filled, and sweet. You are rejoicing in forgiven sin and loving it. First John 2:12 echoes these feelings, "I write to you, little children, because your sins are forgiven you for His name's sake."

The words of the wonderful old hymn "It is Well With My Soul"[26] come to mind:

> My sin—oh, the bliss of this glorious thought!—
> My sin, not in part but the whole,
> Is nailed to the cross, and I bear it no more,
> Praise the Lord, praise the Lord, O my soul!

Truly, little children are wonderful, but we don't want them to stay little forever. As a grandfather, I love little children, but I see there can be problems. Little children can be lazy, not helping around the house. They can also be a little rude, even burping in your face. Furthermore, small children can be selfish and uncooperative. They will wake you up in the middle of the night to take care of them.

For example, I have two very young grandsons named Andrew and Stephen Paul. Stephen's parents are missionaries. When their family was home on furlough, Andrew and Stephen were able to meet and play together. It did not go so well. When we put Stephen on the floor to play with Andrew, he crawled over and bit poor Andrew.

Similarly, baby Christians can be a challenge. When they first come to Christ, they have so much to learn. And, they can also be lazy, rude, selfish, and uncooperative. Maturity is needed. Babies have to grow up. It's part of the process.

Honestly, I used to think that a perfect church was where everyone was a mature, spirit-filled, Christ-like Christian. But, that's not a perfect church. That is a failing church. All churches need new converts, new babes in Christ. To be succeeding, a church must be full of spiritual children. Our churches ought to be maternity wards, full of new babies in Christ.

The Triumphant Warfare of Adulthood

The second stage in our spiritual growth is the triumphant warfare of adulthood. From the childhood stage, we move next to the adulthood stage. Look again at the passage in 1 John 2:13-14.

I write to you, fathers, because you have known Him who is from the beginning. I write to you, young men, because you have overcome the wicked one. I write to you, little children, because you have known the Father. I have written to you, fathers, because you have known Him who is from the beginning. I have written to you, young men, because you are strong, and the word of God abides in you, and you have overcome the wicked one.

When we enter the adulthood stage, we become workers and warriors. Our churches are full of workers and spiritual warriors. These are vibrant, healthy, wholesome people who are no longer children, who are no longer having to be served. Workers have learned to serve and to work hard for the Kingdom of God.

In churches around the world, there are workers everywhere you look. Some workers are serving in the nursery, some are directing traffic on the parking lots, and others are working the sound and lights. Many workers sing in the choir, play an instrument, or teach a Bible study class. I'm so thankful for the workers in our churches.

Equally important, there are warriors in our churches. How did they become warriors? The Word of God has made them strong. In 1 John 2:14, we read, "I have written to you, young men, because you are strong, and the word of God abides in you, and you have overcome the wicked one."

Are you one of these workers or warriors? Have you moved from the childhood stage to the adulthood stage? This movement and growth take place as we regularly spend time reading, studying, and hearing the Bible. The Word of God makes you strong. But, the devil wants to keep you in the childlike stage. He doesn't want you to be strong. Nor does he want you to be a worker and a warrior. And because of that, he will try to keep you defeated.

Imagine, if you will, the best high school football team that has ever played. Suppose that the high school team was to have to play against the Tennessee Titans or the Kansas City Chiefs. That wouldn't be fair, would it? If they played hard-nosed football, it would be devastating for the high school team because they're not mature. The pro team would crush them.

Similarly, the devil is like one of those pro teams going up against a high school team. To fight him and stand against him, Christians must grow up and be made strong in the Word of God. That's the only way we are going to defeat Satan and live in victory.

The Tested Wisdom of Parenthood

There's a final stage of spiritual growth; it's the tested wisdom of parenthood. After moving from the childhood stage to the adulthood stage, all believers are to move into the parenthood stage. Read once again the words of John in 1 John 2:13-14:

> I write to you, fathers, because you have known Him who is from the beginning. I write to you, young men, because you have overcome the wicked one. I write to you, little children, because you have known the Father. I have written to you, fathers, because you have known Him who is from the beginning. I have written to you, young men, because you are strong, and the word of God abides in you, and you have overcome the wicked one.

How do we attain this third stage? How do we grow into spiritual parents? We do this by spending time with the Lord and seeking to become more and more like Him. If you spend enough time with someone, you begin to think and act as they do. Some people say that when you've lived together for a long time, you even begin to look alike. I tell you, my wife Joyce is getting worried.

We become spiritual parents by pressing in close to Jesus and becoming more like Him. As we look, think, and act more like

Him, we will start to reproduce spiritual children. Indeed, spiritual parents reproduce through soul winning and discipleship. Are you reproducing yourself spiritually? Does anyone consider you to be their spiritual mother or father?

Spiritual parents also provide for the needs of others. When a mature believer sees a need, they seek to help. To the church, they tithe generously. To missionaries, they give freely. To those in despair, they share graciously. Are you a spiritual parent who is providing for the needs of others? Are you sharing what you have so that others might grow and prosper?

The third trait of a spiritual parent is wisdom. Parents have wisdom. Spiritual parents are sought out by others who are struggling or need insights. Do people come to you when they have a heartache, a tear, a fear, or a problem? Do others want to talk over issues with you? If so, it's because you are mature. You have come to the parenthood stage of maturity.

Notice something interesting as well: as you grow in Christ, you don't lose the first two stages of spiritual development. All three stages are legitimate, and a parent is a composite of them all. In a parent, there ought to still be the vision and zeal of a young adult. And in a young adult, there ought to be the wonder of childhood. You don't grow away from one stage to another. Rather, you just add each stage to the mix.

Now, if you're perfectly whole, all of those will be in you. Do you know who makes the best youth workers? These people still have youth in them. They can think and identify with young people because that's still in them.

Who are the people that you would enjoy being around the most? Well, I'll tell you, people like my dad. My daddy had a little boy in him. He always wanted to play; he never grew out of that, never became old and grumpy. Correspondingly, there ought to be a little boy in every man, and there ought to be a young man in every man, and there ought to be a father in every man. All three can exist together in a mature believer.

A great example of the maturing of a believer is the Apostle John. When John first got saved, he was mean, and he stayed that way for a while till he grew. John had a violent disposition. Mark 3:17

tells us that his nickname was, "Son of Thunder." In other words, John was a violent man with a hair-trigger temper.

The Apostle John was also a self-seeking man. We read this in Mark 10:37 when he went to Jesus with the other disciples and asked, "Grant us that we may sit, one on Your right hand and the other on Your left, in Your glory." John was in the middle of this heated argument about who was going to be the greatest in the kingdom. Selfishly, he sought after power and position, along with many of the other disciples.

Another childish trait of John's was prejudice. One time, Jesus and John were going through Samaria, and the Samaritans didn't treat Jesus very well. In Luke 9:54-55, we read, "And when His disciples James and John saw this, they said, 'Lord, do You want us to command fire to come down from heaven and consume them, just as Elijah did?' But He turned and rebuked them, and said, 'You do not know what manner of spirit you are of.'"

As John saw Jesus being mistreated. He said, "I'll tell you what, God, let's nuke them. I'll tell you what, Jesus, let's get a little heavenly napalm and fry them because of the way that they're acting." Jesus said, "John, you don't know what spirit you're of." Jesus had to rebuke John for his words of prejudice.

Another childlike trait of John's was his intolerance. In Luke 9:49 we read, "Now John answered and said, 'Master, we saw someone casting out demons in Your name, and we forbade him because he does not follow with us.'" In their little holy huddle, John did not want some stranger to join, some outsiders to become part of their religious group.

Truly, you would not have wanted to drive across the country with this guy named John before he grew up in the Lord. He was saved, but he was a mess. Jesus enlisted John as a disciple—knowing what a mess he was. And, as John grew in the Lord, he was no longer selfish. When he wrote the Gospel of John, he mentioned a disciple that Jesus loved, but he never entered his own name. Even though he was talking about himself, he would just write, "Now there was leaning on Jesus' bosom one of His disciples, whom Jesus loved" (John 13:23).

Also, John grew into a man who no longer tried to take the best seat in the house. He matured out of his prejudice as well. Consider the example of his trip to Samaria in Acts 8:14-15: "Now when the apostles who were at Jerusalem heard that Samaria had received the word of God, they sent Peter and John to them, who, when they had come down, prayed for them that they might receive the Holy Spirit."

The first time he visited Samaria, John said, "Lord, let fire come down upon them." The second time he said, "Oh, God, bless these people. Fill them with the Holy Spirit." He's no longer prejudiced and no longer intolerant. As a matter of fact, he's the one who wrote in this same book, 1 John 1:7, "But if we walk in the light as He is in the light, we have fellowship with one another, and the blood of Jesus Christ His Son cleanses us from all sin." John was changed. To be sure, he was transformed.

THE MEANS OF MATURITY

Shifting gears a little, let's think about the means of maturity. We've considered the marks of maturity as we move from childhood to young adulthood to parenthood.

Now, let's examine some of the means to get to maturity. All of us need to grow up and become strong in the Lord. But, it is a process, a series of steps that we must take to get there. First, there is the miracle of life, the place where you meet Christ and begin to grow.

Years ago, we were trying to teach this concept to the children in our church. We gave all of the children a small potted plant. Each plant was the same as the others. Then, we instructed most of the children to give the plant water, sunlight, and fertilizer. However, a few of the groups of children, we told them not to give their plants all of these ingredients. One group withheld water, another sunlight, and the third fertilizer.

At the end of the experiment, we invited all of the children to bring their plants together for comparison. The plants that received sunlight, water, and fertilizer looked great and were flourishing. But, the other plants all had issues; some were rather yellow, and others had leaves drooping. The experiment proved that healthy plant growth involves sunlight, water, and fertilizer. We were also trying to teach the kids a spiritual lesson about what it means to grow in the grace and knowledge of Jesus Christ.

There was one final group in the plant research that we conducted with the children. To this final group, we offered a dead stick. We told them to water it, give it sunlight and fertilizer. However, that dead stick didn't grow because it was dead. Similarly, for you to grow, you have to cease being a dead stick. You have to get saved. You have to be born again and receive Jesus. There's the miracle of life.

Also, there's a second step in the means of maturity. This step can frustrate some of us. Simply put—spiritual growth takes time. To mature in the Lord, there must be the passing of time. There is no instant maturity. It's just not set up that way. God wants you to grow in the grace and knowledge of our Lord and Savior Jesus Christ. And, the secret of maturity is spending time with the Lord knowing you are not going to be mature overnight.

Thirdly, to move toward maturity, there must be nourishment. You're going to have to feed on the Word of God. In 1 John 2:14, John reminds them, "I have written to you, young men, because you are strong, and the word of God abides in you."

In 1 Peter 2:2, we read, "As newborn babes, desire the pure milk of the word, that you may grow thereby." There is no way possible on God's green earth that you can grow without taking in nourishment, and your nourishment is the Word of God.

Ethel Barrett, a beloved Christian storyteller, talked about the spiritual growth of Dwight L. Moody.

When Dwight L. Moody became a Christian, he developed such a hunger for God's Word, spent so much time reading it, and was so quick to obey it that he became a menace to other believers. His rapid spiritual growth was an embarrassment to certain people, though they had been saved for years and never grew up in Christ. Week after week the church Moody attended . . . he would share a new experience that he'd had with the Lord. Finally, some of the older saints just couldn't stand being humiliated anymore by his life, and they went to his uncle and asked him if he could slow him down and tone him down because he was just feeding on the Word of God, devouring the Word of God, and then he was obeying the Word of God.

And then Ethel Barrett went on to say this about Moody:

His robust, spiritual health and abounding energy disturbed their napping. He was just too much. So while they were sucking their thumbs, he was growing until he left them far behind. He grew more in a few years than they did in twenty.[27]

Isn't that amazing? The Word of God. Moody got hold of the Word of God and he devoured it.

I read one time where Moody said, "You know, I used to pray to God for faith. One day, I read in the Bible where faith comes by hearing, and hearing by the Word of God. That's the secret. If I want faith, I've got to let the Word of God come into me."[28] Moody stopped praying for faith and asked God to give him an understanding of the Bible, and he said he grew in faith.

Years ago, there was another famous preacher from Bristol, England. His name was George Mueller. If you read about the life of Mueller, it's a life of miracle after miracle after miracle. Indeed, he was a great prayer warrior. And, he shared the secret to his prayer life and maturity.

When I come to my quiet time, I just greet the Lord for a few moments and then I get into the Word of God. I study the Word of God. I devour the Word of God. I let the Word of God fill me. The first thing I did after having asked in a few words the Lord's blessings upon His precious Word, was to begin to meditate on the Word of God, searching, as it were, into every verse to get a blessing out of it, not for the sake of the public ministry of the Word, not for the sake of preaching on what I had meditated upon, but for the sake of obtaining food for my own soul.[29]

What does he mean by the phrase *food for my own soul*? Not prayer, but the Word of God. And, not simply reading the Bible so that it only passes through your mind, just as water runs through a pipe, but considering what you read, pondering over it, and applying it to your heart.

These words from George Mueller sound much like the words found in Jeremiah 15:16: "Your words were found, and I ate them, and Your word was to me the joy and rejoicing of my heart; for I am called by Your name, O LORD God of hosts." In other words, Jeremiah says, "Lord, I devoured Your Word. I fed on Your Word."

How do most people read the Bible? For many, the Bible is like a recipe book for us to look at, but we never prepare or eat the meal.

One man said to his wife, "Why do you call it shopping; you never buy anything?"

She said, "Why do you call it fishing; you never catch anything?"

Truly, some people window shop through the Bible. They pull out a good verse and hang it on the refrigerator or share it on social media, but they never let the words get deep into their hearts. We need to feed on the Word of God. That's what Mueller and Moody did. When they fed on the Word, then they became mighty in faith.

Finally, we come to a fourth means of spiritual maturity. This fourth principle teaches us that growth demands the discipline of exercise. Hebrews 5:14 puts it this way: "But solid food belongs to those who are of full age, that is, those who because of use have their senses exercised to discern both good and evil." To grow up in the Lord requires that your spiritual senses get exercised. In the physical realm, when the physical body gets exercised, it toughens and hardens.

Sadly, I've been a pastor long enough to know that most Christians are flabby. They have no strength. They have no vitality because they have no exercise. Every Sunday, they go to church and sit and soak, thinking this is enough. But, this is not serving God. The service of Christians begins when you walk out the church doors and go out into the world.

Consequently, when you begin to serve God, you're going to grow. You will grow in the grace and knowledge of our Lord and

Savior Jesus Christ. And, the more you serve and grow, the stronger you will become spiritually.

You may be a baby Christian, but you can start somewhere. Start reading the Word of God. Don't worry about what you don't understand. Obey what you do understand, and before long you'll be understanding what you didn't understand. And the same thing is true about service. Don't worry about what you can't do. Find out what you can do and begin to do it, and you will grow.

It takes life to grow. It takes nourishment to grow. It takes exercise to grow. But if you are a dead stick, you're not going to grow at all.

Why not pray this prayer as we conclude this chapter:

God, help me to be a growing Christian. You helped the Apostle John to grow. You took this man who was selfish and this intolerant man, this violent man, and You made him into such a wonderful apostle. Lord, You can do that for me. God, I want to be a growing Christian.

ENDNOTES

25. "Thoughts on the Business Side of Life." *Forbes*, Forbes Magazine, www.forbes.com/quotes/7075/.

26. Spafford, Horatio G. "It Is Well With My Soul" 1873.

27. "D. L. Moody: His Life, as Told by Ethel Barrett (Audio CD)." *To*, homeschoolhowtos.com/collections/historical/products/d-l-moody-his-life-as-told-by-ethel-barrett-audio-cd.

28. www.facebook.com/keithferrin. "I Prayed for Faith - DL Moody." *KeithFerrin.com*, keithferrin.com/quotes/prayed-faith-dl-moody/.

29. Mueller, George. "George Mueller on Morning Devotions and Quiet Times." *George Mueller on Personal Devotions and Quiet Times*, www.foundationsforfreedom.net/Topics/Devotions/Devotions020.html.

YOU CAN BE SURE

ROMANS 8:28-31

"Where you may have a question mark about your relationship with Jesus, I want you to be able to exchange it for an exclamation mark."
—Adrian Rogers

Have you ever been in a store and seen a little child who is trying to run up the down escalator? The escalator's coming down and he's just trying to see if he can go up while the steps are going down. Even going with all his might, he cannot ascend the stairs.

That's what it is like for people who are trying to earn salvation by their strength. As they are being tugged at by the downward pull of sin, they are strenuously trying to go higher with their humanitarian efforts. But sin is always greater and stronger than human effort. Most people are simply trying to run up the down escalator toward heaven, and never making it.

That's where grace comes in. We're going to be thinking about grace today and how that grace can give you absolute, rock-solid assurance. The words to Larnelle Harris' song come to mind, *Were It Not for Grace*:

Were it not for grace
I can tell you where I'd be
Wandering down some pointless road to nowhere
With my salvation up to me
I know how that would go
The battles I would face
Forever running but losing this race
Were it not for grace[30]

Look at Romans 8:28 as we begin today: "And we know that all things work together for good to those who love God, to those who are the called according to His purpose." K-N-O-W. You can be sure that you know Christ and experience what I like to call *know-so salvation*. Where you may have a question mark about your relationship with Jesus, I want you to be able to exchange it for an exclamation mark. May you be able to confidently say that you know you are saved and on your way to heaven.

People need assurance of their salvation. I've been in the ministry for a long time; I've never known anybody who was any good to the service of our Lord and Savior Jesus Christ who did not, first of all, have a rock-solid assurance that they're saved and on the way to Heaven. We don't need a hope-so, a maybe-so, think-so, or feel-so salvation. Instead, we can be sure that we are saved. We can enjoy the assurance of our salvation.

Look at the entire passage in Romans 8:28-31.

And we know that all things work together for good to those who love God, to those who are the called according to His purpose. For whom He foreknew, He also predestined to be conformed to the image of His Son, that He might be the firstborn among many brethren. Moreover whom He predestined, these He also called; whom He called, these He also justified; and whom He justified, these He also glorified. What then shall we say to these things? If God is for us, who can be against us?

God is on your side. He is for you. And salvation from start to finish is completely from the Lord. A wonderful old song that illustrates this point is *At Calvary*, written by William R. Newell.

O the love that drew salvation's plan
O the grace that brought
It down to man
O the mighty gulf
That God did span
At Calvary[31]

From our study in Romans 8:28-31, let's consider five foundational facts, five great stones upon which our faith rests. Notice the wording in Romans 8:29: "For whom He foreknew, He also predestined." Then, note the words in Romans 8:30: "Moreover whom He predestined, these He also called." Finally, notice the words in the second part of Romans 8:30: "whom He called, these He also justified; and whom He justified, these He also glorified."

There are five keywords in this passage that are the bedrock of your salvation and the basis of your assurance. I don't want you to miss those wonderful five words of assurance: *foreknowledge, predestination, calling, justification,* and *glorification.*

YOU CAN BE SURE OF GOD'S FOREKNOWLEDGE OF YOUR SALVATION

First, of all, I want you to know that you can be sure of God's foreknowledge of your salvation. What does that mean in plain English? God knew that you were going to be saved before you ever got saved. God foreknew. Indeed, God doesn't learn anything. God already knows everything. We call this God's omniscience.

The Greek word *foreknow* is the word *proginosko.* It's a noun that is the form of the word *prognosis.* When you visit your doctor, he or she will poke around on you and make a prognosis based on investigation and testing. It may be a good prognosis; it may not. But it's just an educated guess that doctors have to make.

I heard about a doctor who told a patient that he only had a year to live. Then, the doctor said, "Your bill to me is $5,000."

The patient exclaimed, "I can't pay it."

So, the doctor answered, "Well, I'll give you another year."

Sometimes the doctor's prognosis is not always correct; it is not always exact. But when God foreknows something, God is not making an educated guess. God knows beyond a shadow of any doubt. That's the reason that sometimes we get confused when we get into things like foreknowledge because we're looking at it from a human vantage point.

Can you imagine a little boy watching a parade through a knothole? He can't even get over the fence to see the parade, so he just sees pieces of that parade as they go past. But then suppose somebody takes the little guy up onto the bleachers to watch the parade. Now, he can see everything—all the bands, all the floats, and everything in between—because he has a different vantage point.

As human beings, we are limited. We're looking at life through a knothole. Do you understand that? But God sees it all. God inhabits all of eternity. God sees the beginning, the middle, and the end. And, God sees it all at one time. Consider this: God saw you getting saved before you ever got saved. God foreknew it. That means that you were in the heart and mind of God before He swung this planet into space.

God chose you and elected you. And, the elect are those who receive Jesus. The elect are the "whoever believes" that we read about in John 3:16. First Peter 1:2 tells us that we are "elect according to the foreknowledge of God the Father, in the sanctification of the Spirit, for obedience and sprinkling of the blood of Jesus Christ."

There was a boy in West Palm Beach, Florida, disobeying his parents, skipping school, cheating in school, using bad language, and getting in fights, but he heard the Gospel and he repented of his sin. He asked Jesus to come into his life and save him. Before God ever made the world, He saw this boy in Florida coming to Christ. That boy was me. Indeed, God saw that boy repenting of his sin and trusting Christ before he ever made the world, and He said, "He's one of My elect." Elect according to the foreknowledge of God; that's what the Bible says.

Now the Bible teaches that God chooses certain people to be elect. John 6:37 says, "All that the Father gives Me will come to Me, and the one who comes to Me I will by no means cast out." That's looking at it from God's viewpoint. Father God looks at things in light of eternity.

As humans, we have a very limited perspective. That's the reason we sometimes get confused. Yes, God has given the elect to the Lord Jesus. God says they will come to Him. And Jesus said they will be received. One day, Jesus will tell the Father that we are all present and accounted for.

But these topics of free will and election can become confusing—especially when we try to put God is a box of our own making. We try to understand the mind of God, and this is just not possible.

If we try to say that it's all up to God, and man has nothing to do with salvation, then we lose our free will. However, if we declare that it's all up to man, and God has nothing to do with it, then we dismiss the sovereignty of God. Truly, it is both. We have free will, and God is completely sovereign.

Your election is based upon God's foreknowledge. Moreover, to *foreknow* does not mean to cause. God did not decide before the foundation of the world to send some to heaven and some to hell. He knows who will accept Him and who will reject Him, but He desires that all will come to Jesus.

Second Peter 3:9 reminds us of this promise: "The Lord is not slack concerning His promise, as some count slackness, but is longsuffering toward us, not willing that any should perish but that all should come to repentance."

Let me present you with a challenging question. Do you believe that everything that is going to happen eventually will? It may sound like a silly statement, but think about it. Everything that is going to happen eventually will. Right? God knows everything that's going to happen. God knows I just scratched my ear, but God knew from eternity I'm going to scratch my ear. Ultimately, God can't learn anything. Not a blade of grass moves without his knowledge.

Indeed, God foreknew that you would receive the Lord Jesus Christ. You are elect according to the foreknowledge of God. That's what the Bible says. Nothing takes God by surprise. He knew when, how, and where you would come to Jesus. He foreknew your salvation. In short, God knew from all eternity who would choose Him and who would not.

YOU CAN BE SURE OF YOUR PREDESTINATION TO BE LIKE JESUS

There's a second keyword in Romans 8:28-31. It's the word *predestination.* You can be sure of your predestination to be like Jesus. Look again at Romans 8:29: "For whom He foreknew, He also predestined to be conformed to the image of His Son, that He might be the firstborn among many brethren."

Predestination doesn't deal with the lost; it deals with the saved. God doesn't predestine some people to go to Hell, and God doesn't predestine some people to go to Heaven. God wants everybody to be saved. Consider the words in 1 Timothy 2:3-6.

> For this is good and acceptable in the sight of God our Savior, who desires all men to be saved and to come to the knowledge of the truth. For there is one God and one Mediator between God and men, the Man Christ Jesus, who gave Himself a ransom for all, to be testified in due time.

God wills that all men should be saved. God is not willing that any should perish. You see, the problem is not that God doesn't want people to be saved. The problem is that God also gives human beings a will. And if God had not given human beings a will, He could not have real fellowship with us.

Look at Matthew 23:37. Jesus is approaching Jerusalem and realizing that the city would be destroyed by Titus, the Roman general. As Jesus comes down the slopes of the Mount of Olives, heading towards Jerusalem, he starts to weep great, salty tears. With a heart broken, He convulsed in sobs, saying, "O Jerusalem, Jerusalem, the one who kills the prophets and stones those who are sent to her! How often I wanted to gather your children together, as a hen gathers her chicks under her wings, but you were not willing!"

It's not God's will that any perish. God would have redeemed the people of Jerusalem. Jesus would have saved them, but they chose not to be saved. Second Corinthians 5:13-15 reiterates this point.

For if we are beside ourselves, it is for God; or if we are of sound mind, it is for you. For the love of Christ compels us, because we judge thus: that if One died for all, then all died; and He died for all, that those who live should live no longer for themselves, but for Him who died for them and rose again.

The Apostle Paul believed that Jesus died for all people to be saved. But, sadly, some people are teaching today that God doesn't want everyone to be saved. Missions and evangelism are unnecessary to these people because they believe God has already determined who will come to Christ. But 1 Timothy 2:3-4 tells us, "For this is good and acceptable in the sight of God our Savior, who desires all men to be saved and to come to the knowledge of the truth."

What does predestination mean then? Predestination means just what it says in Romans 8:29: "For whom He foreknew, He also predestined to be conformed to the image of His Son."

When God saves somebody, God predestines that somebody is going to be just like the Lord Jesus Christ. First John 3:2 reminds us, "Beloved, now we are children of God, and it has not yet been revealed what we shall be, but we know that when He is revealed, we shall be like Him, for we shall see Him as He is."

Predestination is the act of an omnipotent God who has settled the work. What has been settled in Heaven cannot be annulled by Hell or humanity. It is fixed! You're going to become more like Jesus if you're saved. However, if you are not saved, you're going to spend eternity in Hell with the devil. These are the choices that we all have.

YOU CAN BE SURE OF YOUR CALLING TO SALVATION

A third certainty found in Romans 8:29-31 is that you can be sure of your calling to salvation. Look again at Romans 8:29-30:

"For whom He foreknew, He also predestined to be conformed to the image of His Son, that He might be the firstborn among many brethren. Moreover whom He predestined, these He also called; whom He called, these He also justified; and whom He justified, these He also glorified."

Does God call some people to salvation and not call others? No. Whenever the Gospel is preached, God is calling all people to salvation. How does God call us? Through the preaching of the Word. Check out the words of 2 Thessalonians 2:13-14.

> But we are bound to give thanks to God always for you, brethren beloved by the Lord, because God from the beginning chose you for salvation through sanctification by the Spirit and belief in the truth, to which He called you by our gospel, for the obtaining of the glory of our Lord Jesus Christ.

When you believe the truth, that's what makes you a part of the chosen. And how does God call people? By the Gospel, by the preaching of the Gospel of Jesus Christ, and this message is God calling you.

If you've not yet been saved, God wants you to be saved. And how does God call? God calls through the preaching of the Gospel. And this calling, you see, is through sanctification of the Spirit. The Holy Spirit of God takes the Word of God, and God opens the eyes of the blind so he can see what he could not have seen otherwise.

Similarly, God opens the ears of the dead and the deaf that they might hear the Gospel.

A preacher cannot cause conviction or call someone to Jesus. Only the Holy Spirit can do that. It is the Spirit of God that takes the Word of God and sends out the call to the lost. When you hear the Gospel, God is calling you.

Who does God call? Look at Revelation 22:17: "And the Spirit and the bride say, 'Come!' And let him who hears say, 'Come!' And let him who thirsts come. Whoever desires, let him take the water of life freely." If you want to come, you can come. If you have a thirsty heart for Jesus, you can come. If you want to be saved today, God will save you. You are the "whosoever" of John 3:16. Our God calls the lost, wherever they are, and they can come to the Lord Jesus.

By the same token, some people believe that when God calls people, they are not able to resist the call. They call this phenomenon irresistible grace. However, I believe you can resist the call and reject Christ. There are not enough angels in Heaven to drag you down a church aisle to make you follow Jesus.

In Acts 7:51, Stephen is preaching to the religious leaders of his day, and he says, "You stiff-necked and uncircumcised in heart and ears! You always resist the Holy Spirit; as your fathers did, so do you." If the religious leaders of Stephen's day could resist the Holy Spirit, so can we. The Holy Ghost can be resisted.

Earlier we read about the people in the city of Jerusalem resisting Jesus. Matthew 23:37 documents Jesus' words about this resistance, "O Jerusalem, Jerusalem, the one who kills the prophets and stones those who are sent to her! How often I wanted to gather your children together, as a hen gathers her chicks under her wings, but you were not willing!"

In Proverbs 1:22-23, we read this reproof: "How long, you simple ones, will you love simplicity? For scorners delight in their scorning, and fools hate knowledge. Turn at my rebuke; surely I will pour out my spirit on you; I will make my words known to you." God made His words known to the people, and they would not listen. They rejected His truth.

To believe in irresistible grace is to believe in forced love. Forced love is a contradiction in terms. For it to be love, it cannot be forced. Not long ago, I talked to our student ministry about love. I asked them if they wanted to love someone who didn't love them back. All of them wanted to be in a relationship where love was freely offered by both parties.

God Almighty does not force His love on you. You can resist the Holy Spirit if you wish to resist the Holy Spirit. Truly, it's a foolish thing to do. Author C.S. Lewis summed up it up well when he suggested that there are only two kinds of people in life.

> There are only two kinds of people in the end: those who say to God, "Thy will be done," and those to whom God says, in the end, "Thy will be done." All that are in

Hell, choose it. Without that self-choice, there could be no Hell. No soul that seriously and constantly desires joy will ever miss it. Those who seek find. Those who knock it is opened.[32]

In the book of Isaiah, we read an interesting story about Satan. Look at what Satan says in Isaiah 14:13-14: "For you have said in your heart: 'I will ascend into heaven, I will exalt my throne above the stars of God; I will also sit on the mount of the congregation on the farthest sides of the north; I will ascend above the heights of the clouds, I will be like the Most High.'" Satan is vaunting himself. Basically, Satan told Almighty God that he wanted to do his own will, not God's.

When Jesus knelt to pray in the Garden of Gethsemane, He surrendered His will to God's will. When Jesus prayed in Luke 22:42, he prayed, "Father, if it is Your will, take this cup away from Me; nevertheless not My will, but Yours, be done."

There are two categories of people in this world: those who are willing to give their lives to Christ and those who are not. Either we will choose to live for Jesus, or we will choose to live for ourselves. It is completely our decision. God does not want you to go to hell, but He has given you free will. You get to decide—to embrace the call to salvation or to reject it.

YOU CAN BE SURE OF YOUR SETTLED JUSTIFICATION IF YOU RECEIVE THE LORD JESUS CHRIST

There's a fourth foundational fact found in Romans 8:28-31. You can be sure of your settled justification if you receive the Lord Jesus Christ. Look again in Romans 8:30: "Moreover whom He predestined, these He also called; whom He called, these He also justified; and whom He justified, these He also glorified."

What is justification? Justification is an act of God where He declares those who've received Jesus Christ righteous. This does not mean that they have earned righteousness. It means that righteousness has been given to them, apart from anything that they have done to deserve it. Justification is all about trusting in the finished work of Jesus Christ on the cross.

Look with me to Romans 4:5: "But to him who does not work but believes on Him who justifies the ungodly, his faith is accounted for righteousness." Did you see that? Your faith is counted for righteousness.

Of course, justification is more than a pardon for your sins. It's more than an acquittal. Justification means that you are not only pardoned; but that God—by a forensic act of His love and His divine righteousness—declares you righteous, apart from works of any kind. Justification has nothing to do with good behavior, baptism, or keeping commandments. Rather, we trust in the finished work of Christ on the cross.

What is the basis of this justification? It is the blood of Jesus Christ. Romans 5:9 tells us, "Much more then, having now been justified by His blood, we shall be saved from wrath through Him." The only way that you can be justified is through the precious blood of the Lord Jesus Christ on Calvary's cross. Our good deeds, emotions, intuition, and possessions are not enough. Nothing we own or do can justify us.

If you could be saved by any other way, then Jesus Christ would never have died on bloody Calvary. Your sin will be pardoned in Christ or punished in Hell, but it'll never be pardoned. Surely, you'll never be justified apart from the blood of Christ.

How does justification become effective? It comes into effect when you trust Jesus. Look at Romans 3:4: "As it is written: 'That You may be justified in Your words and may overcome when You are judged.'" In Romans 4:5, we read, "But to him who does not work but believes on Him who justifies the ungodly, his faith is accounted for righteousness." And, in Romans 5:1, we read, "Therefore, having been justified by faith, we have peace with God through our Lord Jesus Christ."

What are the results of this justification? Consider the words of Romans 4:5-8.

But to him who does not work but believes on Him who justifies the ungodly, his faith is accounted for righteousness, just as David also describes the

99

blessedness of the man to whom God imputes righteousness apart from works: blessed are those whose lawless deeds are forgiven, and whose sins are covered; blessed is the man to whom the Lord shall not impute sin.

God will never again put sin on your record when you get justified. If God put sin on your record, you'd be lost again. One half of one sin would take you to Hell. Does that mean, therefore, that you can sin and not worry about it? Not at all. God punishes sin. Hebrews 12:6 warns us, "For whom the LORD loves He chastens, and scourges every son whom He receives."

However, God deals differently with His children than He does with the lost. Once you become His child, He will discipline you. But the Bible also says, "Blessed is the man to whom the Lord shall not impute sin" (Romans 4:8).

That's justification, friend, and it's glorious. Romans 8:33 encourages us, "Who shall bring a charge against God's elect? It is God who justifies." You can be certain that your justification is provided through the blood of Jesus Christ.

YOU CAN BE SURE OF YOUR ETERNAL GLORIFICATION

There is one final foundational fact I'd like to mention. You can be sure of your eternal glorification. Look at Romans 8:30 once again: "Moreover whom He predestined, these He also called; whom He called, these He also justified; and whom He justified, these He also glorified."

God, in His eternity, saw you as a lost sinner. You came under conviction and received Jesus. God saw this happen. Then, He watched you grow in your sanctification. And, He sees you already in heaven. He sees all of this happening now. Time and space do not limit God.

This is why we have eternal security. What's been settled in heaven cannot be annulled and undone in time. What a marvelous future is ours!

Now, what does all of this mean for you? If you'll put your faith in the Lord Jesus Christ, you can be sure that you are His.

Let's close with wonderful words from the old hymn, *Have Faith in God*:

> Have faith in God, He's on His throne
> Have faith in God, He watches o'er his own
> He cannot fail, He must prevail
> Have faith in God, have faith in God[33]

ENDNOTES

30. "Larnelle – Were It Not For Grace." *Genius*, genius.com/Larnelle-were-it-not-for-grace-lyrics.

31. "Hymn: At Calvary." *Hymnalnet RSS*, www.hymnal.net/en/hymn/h/342.

32. "A Quote from The Great Divorce." *Goodreads*, Goodreads, www.goodreads.com/quotes/16309-there-are-only-two-kinds-of-people-in-the-end.

33. *Lyrics to Have Faith In God - Hymn Lyrics Search - Name That Hymn*, namethathymn.com/hymn-lyrics/viewtopic.php?t=424.

BIBLE BAPTISM

MATTHEW 28:18-20

"When we go down into those baptism waters and come back out, we are a beautiful picture of the death, burial, and resurrection of Jesus."
—Adrian Rogers

Have you heard of the Great Commission? The mandate for the Great Commission is found in Matthew 28:18-20. This is where we find out what the Lord Jesus Christ gave as marching orders to the church, her Great Commission.

Jesus had a brief ministry; His public ministry lasted only a little over three years. How did Jesus begin His ministry? Jesus began His ministry by being baptized by John in the River Jordan. How did Jesus conclude His ministry? Jesus concluded His ministry by commanding the practice of baptism.

Look at Matthew 28:18-20.

And Jesus came and spoke to them, saying, "All authority has been given to Me in heaven and on earth. Go therefore and make disciples of all the nations, baptizing them in the name of the Father and of the Son and the Holy Spirit, teaching them to observe all things that I have commanded you; and lo, I am with you always, even to the end of the age." Amen.

Jesus is here today, He is still speaking, and He is still saying the same thing. His mandate has not changed. There's no stutter, no stammer, no apology, and no equivocation in Jesus' words. It is written in the Word of God. We're to lead people to Christ, baptize them and teach them to observe everything He has commanded us. Now that's what the Word of God says—clearly written in black print on white paper.

Let's talk about baptism today, but not Baptist baptism. Instead, let's talk about the Bible doctrine of baptism. What does the Bible teach about baptism? What does it look like? How are we to do it? And what does Jesus tell us about baptism? Jesus has all authority, and we need to understand and heed what He teaches us about baptism.

THE BIBLICAL METHOD OF BAPTISM

What is the method of baptism? In Mark 1:9-10, we see the example of how Jesus was baptized. "It came to pass in those days that Jesus came from Nazareth of Galilee and was baptized by John in the Jordan. And immediately, coming up from the water, He saw the heavens parting and the Spirit descending upon Him like a dove."

Jesus traveled 60 miles in one direction to be baptized. Jesus went from Nazareth to Jordan and was baptized by John the Baptist in the Jordan River. The Bible also says that He came up from out of the water. This verse suggests that He was down in the water and had to be brought up out of the water. Thus, the Bible shows us that Jesus was baptized by immersion.

Why was John baptizing in the Jordan River? Look at John 3:23 to see why Jesus chose this particular location: "Now John also was baptizing in Aenon near Salim, because there was much water there. And they came and were baptized." The word *baptized*, as you've heard, means immersed.

The reason that John went out to the River Jordan was not for the scenery, nor for the convenience. Indeed, it takes a lot of water to baptize. If I baptized the way some people do baptism, I could baptize a large group of people with a bucket full of water and have plenty left over. But baptism takes much water. The Jordan River was a muddy, old river and it wasn't convenient, but there was much water there.

Years ago, I traveled to Kenya in East Africa to visit a missionary friend. We drove out in a Land Rover to meet with a tribe of Maasai warriors. Many of these warriors had been led to faith in Christ and wanted to be baptized. How would my friend baptize them?

When we got to the village, the missionaries took shovels and dug a grave. Then, they lined that grave with plastic sheeting, hauled in water to fill up the grave. One by one, those Maasai warriors were laid in that muddy water, in that grave, symbolizing that they had died with the Lord Jesus Christ and were buried with the Lord Jesus Christ.

It is not always easy to baptize by immersion. I remember the first person I ever baptized. Her name was Willie Verene. She was a woman I had led to Christ in a little church I pastored in Fellsmere, Florida. On a Saturday night, I went to see Willie and shared Christ with her. She was open, but not ready to trust Jesus yet. I prayed for her and told her I'd come back the next day.

The next day, as she opened her door, I could tell that something was different. Her face was like the noonday sun. She had given her heart to Christ and wanted to be baptized. But I was a young preacher, and I didn't know how to baptize. Plus, we didn't have a baptistry in our church. We didn't even have running water or a bathroom in our little building on the edge of the Everglades in Florida.

To settle the issue, we decided to use a canal near the church called Lateral A Canal. It was a ditch used to drain the sugar cane fields. So, we headed out to Lateral A Canal with our little church and Willie. She and I slipped down the muddy bank into the cold water. Right there, in the middle of the mud, bugs, and wildlife, I laid that gracious lady back into the water and raised her up. I'll never forget it.

Why did we do it? It'd be so much easier to take a rose petal and put a little water on her head. So, why did we immerse ourselves into that dirty water and baptize Willie? Because we wanted to follow the model of the Lord Jesus. Jesus went all the way to the Jordan River because there was much water there.

On another occasion, we were set to have a baptism service at a different church I pastored in Florida. But, when I arrived to get ready, the baptistry was empty. The janitor had forgotten to turn on the water, and it would take hours to fill the baptismal pool.

What were we going to do? We had people coming from out of town to see folks baptized. At that moment, I had an idea—I believe, a divine inspiration. I called the fire department and told them I had an emergency and needed them to send the pumping truck. They must have thought the church was on fire because they came. In just a few minutes, they had filled the baptistry so I could baptize those people.

Now, why go to all that trouble? Because we wanted to follow the command of Jesus in Matthew 28:19-20: "Go therefore and make disciples of all the nations, baptizing them in the name of the Father and of the Son and the Holy Spirit, teaching them to observe all things that I have commanded you."

Baptism is not a matter of convenience; it's a matter of conviction. However, today, churches are getting so lax and not wanting to go to the trouble of immersing converts. Bible baptism involved immersion. The very word *baptism* is an untranslated Greek word: *baptizo* means to dip, to submerge, to immerse. The Greek word *rantizo* means to sprinkle, and the Greek word *luo* means to pour.

The Bible says that we are to "baptiz[e] them" (Matthew 28:19). If you were to take the word *baptize* from the Greek language and put it into the English language, the word means to dip or to immerse.

Additionally, in the early years, all Christians were baptized by immersion. If you go to Europe and look in some of the great cathedrals that were built before the 13th century, you'll find that they had baptistries where people were immersed. This is the Bible model for baptism, to fully immerse in a pool of water.

THE BIBLICAL MEANING OF BAPTISM

The method and the meaning of baptism are inextricably interwoven. And the reason that the method is so important is that it is connected to the meaning. What is the meaning? Baptism pictures the saving work of the Lord Jesus Christ.

Look at Romans 6:4: "Therefore we were buried with Him through baptism into death, that just as Christ was raised from the dead by the glory of the Father, even so, we also should walk in newness of life." Baptism is a burial. Look at the description given in verses 5-7.

> For if we have been united together in the likeness of His death, certainly we also shall be in the likeness of His resurrection, knowing this, that our old man was crucified with Him, that the body of sin might be done away with, that we should no longer be slaves of sin. For he who has died has been freed from sin.

What does baptism picture? Baptism pictures the Gospel. What is the Gospel? First Corinthians 15:3-4 explains it this way: "For I delivered to you first of all that which I also received: that Christ died for our sins according to the Scriptures, and that He was buried, and that He rose again the third day according to the Scriptures."

Can you understand why the devil would like to destroy that symbolism? If there's one message you'd want to take out of the church, what would be it be? The Gospel. What one message would you want to obliterate? The Gospel. What one message would you want to make sure was not seen over and over again? It is the Gospel: the death, burial, and resurrection of Jesus Christ.

Some will say that the method is not important. But the method does matter. Baptism is a clear picture of a death, a burial, and a resurrection. When we go down into those baptism waters and come back out, we are a beautiful picture of the death, burial, and resurrection of Jesus. God wants it to be clear and God wants it to be plain. That is why we practice baptism by immersion.

The words to the song *Glorious Day* come to mind:

> Living, He loved me
> Dying, He saved me
> Buried, He carried my sins far away

Rising, He justified freely forever
One day He's coming
Oh glorious day, oh glorious day[34]

That is what baptism pictures. It shows, first of all, that we believe that, and that we identify ourselves with Jesus. Look at Romans 6:5: "For if we have been united together in the likeness of His death, certainly we also shall be in the likeness of His resurrection."

When I go under the water, when I'm baptized, it illustrates my death. I die—the old person dies. Because when Jesus died, He died for me. When I trust Him, His death has my name on it. He died my death, He took my place upon that cross, so my death with the Lord Jesus Christ is pictured in baptism.

That's the reason if you were baptized before you got saved, you weren't really baptized. To be baptized before you're saved is like having your funeral before you die. Baptism is a picture of your death. In the Bible, baptism follows salvation. It signifies dying to your old way of living.

Consider a few scriptures. First, look at Acts 2:47: "Praising God and having favor with all the people. And the Lord added to the church daily those who were being saved." You see, you've got to receive the Word before you're baptized. That's why we don't baptize little infants.

Look at Acts 10:46-47: "For they heard them speak with tongues and magnify God. Then Peter answered, 'Can anyone forbid water, that these should not be baptized who have received the Holy Spirit just as we have?'" In this transitional period of the church, the mark that these Gentile believers had received the Holy Ghost was the ability to speak in foreign languages. It was a supernatural gift of God to confirm that the Gospel was going to the Gentiles.

When Peter saw this, he said, "Can anyone forbid water, that these should not be baptized who have received the Holy Spirit just as we have?" Why did he say this? Because you must be saved and receive the Holy Spirit before you're baptized.

In another instance, Paul and Silas were in prison and there was an earthquake. The jailer got saved and came to them wanting to know what he had to do to be saved. In Acts 16:31, Paul and

Silas told the jailer, "Believe on the Lord Jesus Christ, and you will be saved, you and your household." That doesn't mean they'd be saved because he believed; it means they believe the family would be saved just as the jailer was saved.

Now notice what they did after the jailer was saved. Look with me in Acts 16:31-34.

So they said, "Believe on the Lord Jesus Christ, and you will be saved, you and your household." Then they spoke the word of the Lord to him and to all who were in his house. And he took them the same hour of the night and washed their stripes. And immediately he and all his family were baptized. Now when he had brought them into his house, he set food before them; and he rejoiced, having believed in God with all his household.

In all of the examples from scripture that I've mentioned, baptism always follows belief. The Bible never puts baptism before belief. Real baptism follows real salvation. We are buried, then we are raised up. See Romans 6:4 again: "Therefore we were buried with Him through baptism into death, that just as Christ was raised from the dead by the glory of the Father, even so, we also should walk in newness of life."

So when I went down beneath that water—that was a liquid tomb. The old Adrian died with Jesus. The old Adrian is buried. It was a funeral. The only mourner there was the devil. He hated to see me die. I am buried with Jesus. His death had my name on it. He died for me; I died with Him.

Baptism says that the old man is dead. The world is crucified to me, and I'm dead to this world. Goodbye, old world! Goodbye, old man! Hello, new world. Hello, Jesus. Hello, resurrection life. And that's what it's about. When Jesus died, I died. When He arose, I arose. He did that for me and I did that with Him.

Baptism also pictures the fact that one of these days, I'm going to die physically. They are going to lay me in the grave. There will be a funeral, but I won't be there. I'll be up in heaven looking down on you. My body will be in the good clean earth until the trumpet sounds and the resurrection comes. Just like I came up out of the water of the baptistry when I was baptized, I'm coming up out of that grave. My body will be raised. That's what baptism pictures.

Also, baptism pictures Calvary because we died with Jesus. It pictures Easter because we rose with Him. It pictures the Second Coming because one of these days, we're going to be raised up out of that grave to live with the Lord Jesus Christ in a resurrected body.

Don't you think the devil would like to take that picture out of the church?

THE BIBLICAL MOTIVES OF BAPTISM

I'd like to mention the third facet of baptism. It's the Biblical motive of baptism. Why should a person be baptized? I'd like to give you three reasons for Biblical baptism.

Master to Confess

First, we are baptized because there is a Master to confess, the Lord Jesus. We are baptized in the name of the Father, the Son, and the Holy Ghost. We take the name of Jesus. He is now our Master.

The Bible teaches this principle. Look in Romans 6:6: "Knowing this, that our old man was crucified with Him, that the body of sin might be done away with, that we should no longer be slaves of sin." We have a new Master and a new life. We now identify ourselves with Christ. Baptism is your way of saying, "I am not ashamed of Jesus Christ. I thank God for what He did for me on that cross."

On my left hand, I wear a wedding ring. Do you know who gave me this ring? My sweet wife, Joyce. Why do I wear it? Because I love my wife and I'm not ashamed of her. I want everybody to know that I belong to one woman. This ring doesn't make me married. I could be married and not have a wedding ring. But my ring lets everyone know that I am married, and I belong to Joyce.

Similarly, baptism doesn't make you a Christian. But, baptism does publicly show everyone that you belong to Jesus. He is the Master that you confess when you go down into the waters of baptism.

A little boy was saved in the children's church. The teachers told him to go over to the big church and let the pastors know so that he could get baptized. He didn't understand baptism. But he went to the big church and told the pastor, "I've been saved, I need to get advertised." That's what baptism is. Your relationship with Jesus being advertised.

Message to Convey

There's a second reason to be baptized. We are baptized because there is a message to convey. Did you know that whenever you get baptized you're preaching the Gospel? Every time, when a person is baptized, he or she is preaching the Gospel: the death, burial, and resurrection of Jesus Christ. Your baptism conveys what Jesus has done in your life.

Many times, I've seen people saved during a baptism service. As they watch someone else being baptized, they come under conviction of their sins. The very things that baptism pictures are what bring conviction to their hearts.

Mandate to Complete

A final reason to be baptized is the mandate to complete. Look back at Jesus' words in Matthew 28:19-20, "Go therefore and make disciples of all the nations, baptizing them in the name of the Father and of the Son and the Holy Spirit, teaching them to observe all things that I have commanded you; and lo, I am with you always, even to the end of the age."

What is your response to that? *Yes, Lord.*

Have you been baptized? Were you baptized after you were saved? If not, why not talk to one of the pastors at your church and let them know you'd like to experience believer's baptism?

ENDNOTES

34. "Glorious Day (Living He Loved Me) (Lyrics) + Casting Crowns." *Casting Crowns Official Website + Only Jesus Available Now*, castingcrowns.com/ music/glorious-day-living-he-loved-me/.

HOW TO HAVE A MEANINGFUL QUIET TIME

PSALM 119:97-104

*"Your spiritual train is going to run on two rails—revelation and obedience.
If either rail stops, your train stops."*
—Adrian Rogers

C hristianity is not a legal relationship; it is a love relationship.
And people who are legalists never have victory. Ten
thousand "don'ts" will never make you one *iota* more like the
Lord Jesus Christ. But friend, it is Jesus himself who makes you
like Him. You need to personally spend time with Jesus Christ.
In essence, Christianity is a love relationship.

Truly, you cannot love someone that you do not know. And
you cannot know someone that you don't spend quality time with.
To know Him is to love Him. To love Him is to trust Him. To trust
Him is to obey Him. And to obey Him is to be blessed.

To know Jesus is to love Him. You cannot know Jesus
without loving Him. And to love him is to trust Him. You cannot
trust someone you do not love. And trust Him is to obey Him.

The reason we don't obey is that we don't trust. And to obey Him is to be blessed. And it all begins with a quality quiet time, daily communication with the Lord.

Let's look at Psalm 119:97-104.

> Oh, how I love Your law! It is my meditation all the day. You, through Your commandments, make me wiser than my enemies; for they are ever with me. I have more understanding than all my teachers, for Your testimonies are my meditation. I understand more than the ancients because I keep Your precepts. I have restrained my feet from every evil way, that I may keep Your word. I have not departed from Your judgments, for You Yourself have taught me. How sweet are Your words to my taste, sweeter than honey to my mouth! Through Your precepts I get understanding; therefore, I hate every false way.

I'd like to share with you what others have taught me and also some things I've learned in my pilgrimage about having a quality quiet time. I want to give you about five factors, and they'll be easy to remember because they will begin with the letter "P."

YOU MUST HAVE A PROPER PERIOD

First of all, to have a meaningful quiet time, you must have a proper period. You must choose the right time to meet with God. When should you have your quiet time? Here are two keys. First, it should be the very best time of the day for you. Second, it should be early in the day. Rather than giving God the leftovers at the end of the day, why not give Him the first minutes of your day?

For the most effective quite time, plan for at least 30 minutes. You will have to make this time happen. The devil will do everything in his power to prevent you from spending time with the Lord. When you study the life of the Lord Jesus, you find that Jesus made time to be alone with the Father. He—amid a very busy ministry—would withdraw by Himself and be alone with God.

To follow Jesus' example, a quiet time ought to be in the morning. Psalm 5:3 says, "My voice You shall hear in the morning, O Lord; in the morning I will direct it to You, and I will look up." Why in the morning? Well, obviously because you're getting ready to live the day.

Think about it—you don't take the trip and then read the map, do you? You don't get the car tuned after you have taken the trip. And any athlete knows that a great start ensures a great finish. You don't pray for your daily bread after the day is over. Morning prayer unlocks the key to your morning. It's a time to get started with God.

You may not feel like you have time in the morning to have a quiet time. But we do have time if we make time. It's just a matter of determining to do so. For some of you who are efficiency experts, you may feel that a morning quiet time is a waste of time. However, think about a person going out to chop wood. Wouldn't it be time well-spent to sharpen the ax before they begin to chop? If you're going to read a book, are you wasting time when you turn on the light?

God's Word is a lamp to light the way. It's a map to show the way. It is a tool that we work with along the way. And so, you must make time to be with the Lord each morning.

For me, the best time is after breakfast. Generally, I wake up at about 6:00. But I never want to get up. It's a resurrection every morning for me to get out of the bed. It's just the way I am wired. Maybe you are as well. I'm a bit of an owl, a late-night person.

When I wake up in the morning, I stumble into the bathroom and put my knee on the toothpaste to squeeze it. So for me to have my quiet time when I first wake up would be a good cure for insomnia. If I bowed my head and closed my eyes, I'd fall asleep.

Instead, I have to get up, shave, shower, and get ready for the day. I need coffee and breakfast too. Then, Joyce and I'll have a prayer time together at breakfast. We'll pray for our family and try to pray around the world. After this, I retire to my study. This is the best time for me to have time alone with God when my mental acuity is at its best.

Ask God what your best time is to have a quiet time. Then, make this time a matter of priority every day.

YOU MUST HAVE A PROPER PREPARATION

There's a second key to having a meaningful quiet time. Not only must you have the proper period, but you must have the proper preparation. Three things will prepare you for a quiet time.

First, you must be physically alert. I've already mentioned this. You need to find a time when the cobwebs are out of your mind. This will be a time when you can think clearly and when your juices are flowing in your body.

Secondly, you must be morally pure and clean to have a quiet time. Do you know what quiet time is? Quiet time is fellowship with a holy God. The reason that some folks don't have a quiet time is that they feel uncomfortable in God's presence. They don't want to look at God in the face because of the sin in their lives.

What did Adam do after he had sinned, and God came walking in the Garden? Adam fled. Before that, Adam had a quiet time with God, didn't he? Adam and God walked in the Garden; they had fellowship. That was Adam's quiet time, walking in the Garden in the cool of the day. But when there was sin in Adam's life, he did not want to look at God in the face.

If you find in you sometimes a reluctance, maybe even a repugnance to what I'm talking about, it's simply because there may be sin in your life. To have a quiet time, we have to open our hearts for God to purify and clean them. We confess our sins to God, and then we can enjoy fellowship with Him.

Psalm 66:18 teaches us, "If I regard iniquity in my heart, the Lord will not hear." That's a prayer promise. If I regard iniquity in my heart, the Lord will not hear me. In the Sermon on the Mount, Jesus said, "Therefore if you bring your gift to the altar, and there remember that your brother has something against you, leave your gift there before the altar, and go your way. First, be reconciled to your brother, and then come and offer your gift" (Matthew 5:23-24).

Although the previous verse is talking about temple worship, the principle applies to us. We cannot worship God freely if there's a broken relationship in your life that needs to be made right. As God brings relationships to your mind that need mending, mend them.

If we aren't morally pure, can we still have a quiet time? Absolutely, yes! As we begin to pray, we invite God to search our hearts and show us what we need to fix. A great passage to pray as you begin your quiet time is Psalm 139:23-24: "Search me, O God, and know my heart; try me, and know my anxieties, and see if there is any wicked way in me and lead me in the way everlasting."

As you pray, the Holy Spirit may point out something that you need to confess. First John 1:9 says, "If we confess our sins, He is faithful and just to forgive us our sins and to cleanse us from all unrighteousness." There's no reason that any of us should not be as clean, as pure, as the driven snow.

The blood of Jesus Christ, God's Son, cleanses us from all sin. Not some sin, but all sin. Don't let the devil intimidate you by some failure in the past. You have been made clean through the precious blood of Jesus and, by the grace of God, be clean.

So what is the proper preparation? You are physically alert, morally pure, and thirdly, you are mentally aware. This is so important. The Bible tells us to, "Gird up the loins of your mind, be sober, and rest your hope fully upon the grace that is to be brought to you at the revelation of Jesus Christ" (1 Peter 1:13).

What does it mean to "gird up the loins of your mind?" In Bible times, the people wore long flowing robes. If you were to visit Israel today, you'll still see the Bedouins and others wearing these flowing robes. When a man was going to work or fight in Bible days, he would take the loose ends of the robes and tie them around his waist so he wouldn't trip over them. This is what it was to gird up his loins.

Your mind is like that—full of many loose ends. To have a quiet time, you have to get mentally tough. This can be hard for some of us. I know it is for me because I have so many ideas running through my mind. When you and I have a quiet time, we must gather up all of those thoughts and intentionally focus on the Lord.

When our minds want to wander, we have to gird them back up. We have to get serious. We must come with anticipation. Come eagerly. Come expecting to receive something. It's not about emotion. It's about choosing to be tough-minded, focused, and in tune with the Lord Jesus. He's present, and He wants to spend time with you. Your part is to be physically alert, morally pure, and mentally aware.

YOU MUST HAVE A PROPER PLACE

Another key factor in having a meaningful quiet time is to have a proper place for your devotions. Jesus said this about prayer in Matthew 6:6: "But you, when you pray, go into your room, and when you have shut your door, pray to your Father who is in the secret place; and your Father who sees in secret will reward you openly."

Years ago, I went to college with a preacher boy at Stetson University named Judd. When he read Matthew 6:6, he took it very literally. For his quiet time, he would go into his closet, shut the door, and pray. When we couldn't find Judd, we'd go to the closet to look for him. One day, when we couldn't locate Judd, we went to the closet. When we opened the door, he was in there sound asleep on his knees.

What did Jesus mean when He said to enter into your secret place or closet to pray? The word *closet* simply means into a place of isolation. Somewhere where you can shut the door on the world and open the windows to heaven. As you study the life of Jesus, you discover that Jesus was not in a literal closet. But you will find out that Jesus would seek to be alone. Sometimes He'd go out to a mountain. Sometimes He went into the wilderness. At other times, He went into a garden.

A secret place is a sacred place. It's a place where you can have some uninterrupted time alone with the Father. This place should be well-lit and well-ventilated. It should be quiet and free from distractions. Try to avoid all visible and audible distractions. Also, try to find a place where no one will disturb you for a little while.

My favorite place to meet the Lord is in my study at my house. I do work there, but I can also study there. With my books, Bible, and materials close at hand, I can easily enjoy time with the Lord. Incidentally, my wife has a place where she meets with God. It's a little nook where she can be alone and focused on Him.

You also need a place to have a quiet time. Pray and ask God to give you a place. It may be your bedroom. Or, if you have a lot of children in the house, you may have to go into the bathroom and lock the door. Whatever it takes, find a special place to get alone with God.

YOU MUST HAVE A PROPER PROVISIONS

A fourth important factor in having a meaningful quiet time is to have proper provisions. You need to have the right tools. First of all, you need a readable Bible. Make sure the print is large enough and easy enough to read.

If you don't have a good Bible, it's a good time to invest in one. Get a Bible with wide margins and pages made of thick paper. You want something you can wear out with use. I have some Bibles that are decades old. Sometimes I go back and find notes in my Bible, and memories will spring up of things that God taught me in the past. Indeed, you may even want to get more than one Bible. You can have a Bible you take to church and one that you study at home.

It's okay to write, underline, mark, and take notes in your Bible. That's not an irreverent thing to do. Somebody once said the person who has a Bible that is falling apart probably has a life that is not.

A second tool you will want to have for your quiet time is a journal. I have a journal that I use to take notes as I pray, study, and spend time with the Lord. To me, it would be unthinkable to read without a pen in my hand. Instinctively, when I reach for the Bible, I reach for a pen. Why? I expect God to give me something wonderful, and you should too.

You may think that you have a great memory. You'll remember what you read. Who are you kidding? Most of us forget what we read and hear. It is always best to write things down. Writing impresses important facts into our minds. And the weakest ink is better than the best memory. So, get a journal and write in your journal. Expect God to speak to you each morning.

Not only should you have a journal where you write down what God is teaching you, but you also need a prayer journal. I've kept a prayer journal for many years. And I don't use it every morning, but I use it many mornings. This prayer journal reminds me of prayer needs—it helps me to remember who and what to pray for. It contains prayers for family, friends, and church members.

Another helpful tool for you to use during your quiet time is a notepad with a list of things to do for the day. If you will keep this notepad handy, you will be able to make notes while you are having your quiet time. As ideas come to mind, you can pray for them and then note them on your list for the day. Often God will show you things that He wants you to do on that particular day. The notepad helps to keep distractions to a minimum.

Of course, there are other tools you may want to gather. You may find it helpful to have a Bible dictionary, Bible maps, a concordance, and even a commentary or two. For the most part, however, the key quiet time provisions include a readable Bible, a journal, a prayer journal, a pen, and a notepad for daily tasks. With these tools, you can have a wonderful time with the Lord.

YOU MUST HAVE A PROPER PROCEDURE

A final tool for a meaningful quiet time is to have a proper procedure. What is the proper procedure? Is there a best method to follow? May I recommend that the very first thing you do is just get still and get quiet. Psalm 46:10 reminds us, "Be still and know that I am God."

Take a few moments to focus your mind on Him. Calm down, relax, and recognize His presence. You are about to spend time with the King of Kings and Lord of Lords. He is all yours. Let your mind dwell on the fact that Jesus is there with you.

A few years ago, I had a wonderful privilege. I got to teach at The Cove in North Carolina. This is the site of the Billy Graham Learning Center. On one of the evenings, Dr. and Mrs. Graham invited my wife and me to dinner. In a small upper room, the four of us enjoyed a meal together talking about the Lord. It was both a great and humbling experience for us.

But, getting to spend time with the Grahams is nothing compared to the great honor of spending time with Jesus every single morning. He has invited us to be with Him and to enjoy a spiritual meal with Him. We need to fix and focus our minds on this privilege. For the Lord Jesus said, "Lo, I am with you always, even to the end of the age" (Matthew 28:20).

Once you get quiet and focus your thoughts on the Lord, why not lift your hands toward heaven? Look up—with arms raised—and praise Him for a few moments. Recognize Him as Lord. Then, surrender your life to Him. Invite Him to speak to you. Tune your heart to think about the presence of God.

Next, get into the Word of God. I think it's better to start reading the Bible than it is to start in prayer. Read the Word first, and then pray. It is more important for you to hear from God than for God to hear from you. God already knows all about you, but you need to know a lot more about Him. Also, this will tune your heart and get you ready to pray. You hear from God, and then you talk to God in prayer.

As you read the Bible, read for quality and not quantity. Don't see how much of the Bible you can read. Instead, focus on smaller portions. If you are reading the Bible through in a year, you may want to do this at another time in your day. Take your quiet time to think about what you are reading. You might reflect on just one verse discerning what God is saying to you. Read the Bible thoughtfully.

Read the Bible like you would read any other book. Do it sensibly. You don't pick up a book, open it up at random, and start reading in the middle of a paragraph. No, read it sequentially in paragraphs. Use some common sense when you read the Bible.

Also, keep your Bible reading balanced. Read from the Old Testament and read from the New Testament. Read regularly from the Psalms so you learn to worship. Read regularly from the book of Proverbs and gain wisdom.

What about having devotional books? Devotional books are wonderful, but I don't always recommend them for devotion time. Make sure your focus is on the Bible rather than on devotional books. The quiet time is the place where you open the Bible and read intelligently, sequentially, with an open mind, and allow God to speak to you.

After reading, I suggest you meditate on what you are reading. Think about it. I don't mean Oriental meditation or mystical meditation. You focus on the Word of God, meditate on the Word of God, and let the Word of God permeate you.

Here are some questions you can ask as you meditate:

- Is there a command to obey?
- Is there a promise to claim?
- Is there a sin to avoid?
- Is there a lesson to learn?
- Is there a new truth to carry with me?

These are the questions I have written in the flyleaf of my Bible. I refer to them often. As I read, study, and meditate, these questions help me to focus on what specifically God may want to show me each day.

Another thing I do while reading and meditating is write down what God shows me. I take notes in my journal so that I will not forget what I've learned. It doesn't have to be flowery. You're not writing it for publication. You're not writing it to impress other people. Make it intensely personal. And, you'll find yourself sharing these truths with other people. As God gives you nuggets of truth, you'll want to tell others.

At the same time, take that notepad and write down the things that you need to do. Make these your action points for the day. Maybe God will remind you of someone you need to call, email, or text. Maybe He will lead you to give a gift to someone.

Now, you are ready to pray. Pray and pour out your soul to God. Be natural. Don't try to use flowery language when you pray. Jesus instructed us in Matthew 6:7, "And when you pray, do not use vain repetitions as the heathen do. For they think that they will be heard for their many words." Be honest with God. Tell Him how you feel.

As you pray, you may want to refer to your prayer journal. Pray out loud. Sometimes this will help you to stay focused. Try to make complete sentences. Speak clearly, speak plainly. Think about what you are saying when you pray, but don't draw it out. Pray as long as you have a concern on your heart. Don't just keep repeating things like you're going to impress God with the number of words that you say.

Do you ever try to pray and your mind wanders? What can you do about this? Try lifting your hands. This will be like a rebuke to the devil as you lift your arms in victory. And lifting your hands will remind you that you are giving everything back over to God—that thing that's caused your mind to wander, pray about it. Tell God about it. Talk to God about it until you can give it over to Him.

After your quiet time, why not tell someone what God showed you? We ought to meet people and exhort one another. You see, God did not make us to be reservoirs. God made us to be conduits. Some truth God showed you in your quiet time may greatly bless another soul.

Finally, after you spend time with God, obey what He tells you to do. Don't ignore His promptings. Your spiritual train is going to run on two rails—revelation and obedience. If either rail stops, your train stops. Learn to obey the Word of God and when you fail, confess it. Follow through with what He tells you to do each day. You never know how He might use and bless your obedience.

CONCLUSION

Once you start having a quiet time, you may ask how soon will it be before you will see a change in your life? You'll see some change, I believe, right away. But don't expect anything radical and dramatic.

For example, each morning my wife gives me brewer's yeast. She gives me two big tablespoons full of it. And then on top of that, she encourages me to take bee pollen. Also, I take a fist full of vitamins and then 2% milk. We are trying to be healthy at our house.

None of these things makes me feel 100% better in 15 minutes. However, if you'll get on a regimen of eating right, it'll change you.

The same is true of having a daily quiet time. If you'll get on a regimen of obeying the Word of God, getting into the Word of God and feeding your soul, God will change you. The change will not be immediate, and it may not be dramatic, but in the long run, it will change you for eternity.

We all need to have a quality quiet time every day. It will make a tremendous difference in our lives.

HOW TO MAKE YOUR BIBLE COME ALIVE

PSALM 119

"The Bible is not the book of the month nor is it the book of the year.
Rather, the Bible is the book of the ages. It never changes."
—*Adrian Rogers*

I s the Bible a book you love and want to read? Is it essential in your life? A wise man said a long time ago, "These hath God married and no man shall part, dust on the Bible and drought in the heart." [35]

If you do not know, love, understand, practice, and obey the Word of God, I can tell you without stutter, stammer, or apology, you are not a victorious Christian. Today, let's consider how to study the Bible and how to make it come alive in your life. From the pages of Psalm 119, we are going to discover how you can learn to enjoy time in God's Word.

In any realm, knowledge is power. Whether in business, in athletics, or in theology, knowledge is power. If you know good things, you'll do good. And, if you know bad things, you will most likely behave badly. The Bible gives us knowledge so that we might live better lives.

I came across this prayer from someone in Kenya:

From the cowardice that dare not face new truth,
From the laziness that is contented with half-truth,
From the arrogance that thinks it has all truth,
Good, Lord, deliver me.[36]

Truly, I pray that you will not be afraid of the truth. May you and I not be lazy and accept half-truths. May we not be arrogant and think that we need no truth. Instead, may we embrace knowledge and be transformed.

There was a sign in a business that said, "We are not what we think we are; what we think, we are."[37] Did you get that? We're not what we think we are, but rather, what we think, we are. That is, you are what you think. Proverbs 23:7 tells us, "For as he thinks in his heart, so is he." If that is true, if knowledge is power, we need the knowledge of the Word of God to have spiritual power.

Furthermore, we need to be molded, motivated, and managed by the Word of God. However, for so many believers, the Bible remains a closed mysterious book. We say we love the Bible, but we really don't understand it or even read it. There is no cheap, lazy, or magical way to understand the Bible. It must be studied.

Psalm 119 is by far the longest chapter in the Bible, and it is an acrostic in the Hebrew Bible. An acrostic is a special arrangement of letters. Psalm 119 is organized in sections of 22 stanzas. Each stanza starts with a different letter in the Hebrew alphabet. The entire Psalm contains well over a hundred verses; each of these verses deals with the Word of God. The purpose of Psalm 119 is to help us to know and understand the Word of God.

As we look at Psalm 119, I want to point out three main points and several sub-points. If you will practice each of these steps that I will share, I can promise you that you will begin to love the Bible and want to read it more. Practicing these things will make the Bible come alive for you.

YOU MUST APPRECIATE THE VIRTUES OF THE WORD OF GOD

To being with, you must appreciate the virtues of the Word of God. If you don't appreciate these virtues, you are not going to have any desire to learn or study the Bible. Many people do not understand the great value, the great virtue in the Word of God. You must have an appreciation for the Word of God.

Timeless Book

Why should you appreciate the Word of God? First of all, we appreciate the Bible because it is a timeless book. Look at Psalm 119:89 for example: "Forever, O LORD, Your word is settled in heaven."

The Bible is not the book of the month, nor is it the book of the year. Rather, the Bible is the book of the ages. It never changes. Check out Psalm 119:152: "Concerning Your testimonies, I have known of old that You have founded them forever." Forever, God has founded His Word. Look at Psalm 119:160: "The entirety of Your word is truth, and every one of Your righteous judgments endures forever." Other books come and go, but the Bible is here to stay.

Thousands of years have passed since the Bible was written; empires have risen and fallen. Civilizations have changed and re-changed. Science is pushing back the frontiers of knowledge, and yet the Bible stands. There have been emperors who have decreed the extermination of the Bible. Some atheists have laughed and railed at it.

Additionally, some agnostics cynically sneer at the Bible. Some liberals have moved Heaven and earth to remove the miracles from the Bible. There are many materialists who just simply ignore the Bible. But the Bible stands. One of the ways I know the Bible is the Word of God: it's stood up under so much shoddy preaching. The Bible is settled in Heaven.

One great pastor, Dr. Robert G. Lee, said this about the Bible: "All of its enemies have not torn one hole in its holy vesture, nor stolen one flower from its wonderful garden, nor diluted one drop of honey from its abundant hive, nor broken one string on its thousand-stringed harp, nor drowned one sweet word in infidel ink." [38]

First Peter 1:25 puts it this way: "But the word of the LORD endures forever." The Bible is timeless, the Bible is ultimate, and the Bible is indestructible. This is one of the great virtues that makes us love and respect the Word of God—it is a timeless book.

Truthful Book

In the second place, the Bible is a truthful book. Look at Psalm 119:142: "Your righteousness is an everlasting righteousness, and Your law is truth." Now, go to Psalm 119:151: "You are near, O LORD, and all Your commandments are truth." Check out Psalm 119:160 as well: "The entirety of Your word is truth, and every one of Your righteous judgments endures forever."

Do you remember what Pilate asked Jesus when they were talking? In John 18:38, Pilate asked, "What is truth?" In John 17:17, Jesus said, "Sanctify them by Your truth. Your word is truth." In a world that has lost its appreciation for truth, we can say without any hesitation that the Bible is true.

There are some theological experts today who think they ought to re-examine the Bible. Honestly, I think we ought to re-examine any theological experts who feel this way. Of course, there are all sorts of attacks on the truth of the Bible. From the sheer attack of liberals to the most subtle disregard by unbelievers, there is an attack on God's Word.

Perhaps the most insidious attacks are coming from the rear. There is a sort of fringe group of people that wants to take the focus off of the truth of the Bible and place it on life experiences. Rather than concentrate on truth, they want to emphasize their feelings and ideas. Instead of viewing life through the lens of biblical truth, they want to view life through the lens of their perspectives and ideas.

The Apostle Paul had to deal with similar issues in the Church at Corinth. Paul said to them in 1 Corinthians 14:37-38, "If anyone thinks himself to be a prophet or spiritual, let him acknowledge that the things which I write to you are the commandments of the Lord. But if anyone is ignorant, let him be ignorant."

At Corinth, many of the believers had gotten into some charismatic practices. They'd gone crazy over things like speaking in tongues, prophecies, visions, and ecstasies. Paul tried to set things right in his letter to these saints. They were telling him that they had prophetic gifts. His response was, in essence, "If you think you're a prophet, if you think you're spiritual, then you will acknowledge what I say is the Word of God."

And then he says something almost humorous. He said, "But if any man is ignorant, let him be ignorant." He shrugged his shoulders at them, almost saying what many people say today: "It is what it is." In Paul's day and ours, there will be people who want to make the Bible all about their experiences. Truth doesn't matter nearly as much to them as feelings and reality.

There is one more attack on the truth of the Bible, and this one comes from the side. Some don't deny the Bible, but they'd like to prop it up with psychology and philosophy. These people don't believe that the Bible is good enough all by itself. They'd like to add to it.

Second Timothy 3:16 addresses these attackers: "All Scripture is given by inspiration of God, and is profitable for doctrine, for reproof, for correction, for instruction in righteousness."

That word *inspiration* is used only once in the Bible, but what a magnificent word it is. The word is *theopneustos*. It means to be God-breathed (*theo* meaning God, *pneustos* meaning the breath of God).

If you were to pronounce it as it is written, you would say *"pah-newstis,"* much like the word *pneumonia*. We don't say *"pew-monia,"* we say *"pneumonia."* It has to do with breath. This word, *theopneustos*, is talking about the breath of God.

When I speak, *you* hear the breath of Adrian! My lungs have air; my diaphragm is forcing the lungs to expel the air. Then, the air comes up out of my throat, over my larynx, causing my vocal cords to vibrate. My tongue and my teeth and my lips are making sounds. And what you are hearing when I speak is my breath.

The Bible says all Scripture is the breath of God; it is God-breathed. In Matthew 4:4, Jesus said, "Man shall not live by bread alone, but by every word that proceeds from the mouth of God." Jesus was talking about the Bible and how every word of the Bible proceeds from the mouth of God. God has not only breathed into the Scriptures; He has also breathed them out.

Yes, God used men to pen the words of the Bible. Isaiah, Jeremiah, Matthew, and Paul were some of the penmen of God.

They wrote what God led them to write as they heard the voice of God speaking. In 2 Peter 1:21, we read, "For prophecy never came by the will of man, but holy men of God spoke as they were moved by the Holy Spirit." Indeed, the Bible is true because God cannot speak in error.

If you were to go to the Old Testament, you would find phrases like these: "The Word of the Lord" (Psalm 33:4). You will also see references to God speaking, like, "The Lord said" (Genesis 11:6). You will find the phrase, "The Lord said," used 388 times in the Bible. If the Bible is not the very Word of God, it's the biggest bundle of lies that has ever come to planet Earth.

Treasured Book

One final virtue of the Bible that I want you to notice is the fact that the Bible is a treasured book. In Psalm 119:72, we read, "The law of Your mouth is better to me than thousands of coins of gold and silver." The Bible is priceless to me; it is worth more than great piles of gold, silver, rubies, diamonds, bonds, stocks, and cash.

Look at Psalm 119:103: "How sweet are Your words to my taste, sweeter than honey to my mouth!" See also Psalm 119:127: "Therefore I love Your commandments more than gold, yes, than fine gold!" The Bible is a treasured book. The saints and the heroes have pillowed their heads upon the Word of God as they walked through the chilly waters of the river of death.

And the martyrs who died for the witness of Jesus Christ have held the Bible to their chests as the creeping flames came around their feet. In the early church, they loved the Word of God. Those early saints preached it, proclaimed it, pronounced it, and poured it forth like white-hot lava! They loved the Bible, and they trusted it, obeyed it, and claimed it.

Do you know why the Bible is treasured? The words to a familiar song may answer this for you:

Jesus loves me this I know
For the Bible tells me so
Little ones to Him belong
They are weak, but He is strong
Yes Jesus loves me

Yes Jesus loves me
Yes Jesus loves me
The Bible tells me so[39]

Suppose there were buried treasure in your backyard. You'd go down to the hardware store and get a shovel if you don't have one. You'd dig like crazy until you found that treasure. And we should treat the Bible like the amazing treasure that it is. It is a timeless book, it is a truthful book, and it is a treasured book.

WE MUST ASSIMILATE THE VITALITY OF THE WORD OF GOD

Not only must you appreciate the virtues of the Word of God, but you must also assimilate the vitality of the Word of God. The word *vitality* means to be alive. Consider the words of Hebrews 4:12: "For the word of God is living and powerful, and sharper than any two-edged sword, piercing even to the division of soul and spirit, and joints and marrow, and is a discerner of the thoughts and intents of the heart."

God's Word is alive. To be alive is to be full of energy and living. Jesus, speaking to some unbelievers in John 6:63, says, "It is the Spirit who gives life; the flesh profits nothing. The words that I speak to you are spirit, and they are life." The Bible is vital, pulsating with life.

So, how can we assimilate the Word of God? First of all, we can pray over the Word of God. Before we even begin to read and study the Bible, we can pray about our time in the Scriptures. You might pray the words of Psalm 119:12: "Blessed are You, O LORD! Teach me Your statutes." Have you ever prayed that? "Lord God, be my teacher." Pray over your Bible study time and ask God to teach you.

When you pray over it, what will happen? As you pray, your eyes will be opened. In Psalm 119:18, we read, "Open my eyes, that I may see wondrous things from Your law." God will open your eyes and remove the scales so you can read and understand. You may have 20/20 vision, but God has to open your eyes.

Do you remember the story in Luke 24? It is after Jesus' resurrection where He is walking with two disciples on the road to Emmaus. The Bible says that He began to talk to them about the Old Testament, the law and the prophets. A most interesting phrase is mentioned in Luke 24:45: "And He opened their understanding, that they might comprehend the Scriptures." Wouldn't you like for God to do that for you as well?

When you pray over your Bible reading time, your eyes will be opened. In like manner, as you pray over your Bible study, your heart will be stirred. In Psalm 119:36, we read, "Incline my heart to Your testimonies, and not to covetousness." If you don't have a desire for the Word of God, why don't you say, "Oh God, please incline my heart, move my heart, open my eyes, and stir my heart!"

When your eyes are opened and your heart is stirred, then your mind is going to be enlightened. Look at Psalm 119:73: "Your hands have made me and fashioned me; give me understanding, that I may learn Your commandments." Quite often in my sermon preparation, I have put my pencil down, bowed my head, and asked God to give me understanding and wisdom with a passage.

Not only do we pray over Scripture to assimilate it, but we also ponder the Bible. See Psalm 119:15: "I will meditate on Your precepts, and contemplate Your ways." Look also at Psalm 119:147: "I rise before the dawning of the morning, and cry for help; I hope in Your word."

Each morning, we get up and open the Word of God. As we do, we pray and ask God to speak to us and teach us. Then, we sit down with pen and paper, and began to write down and ponder all that God is showing us. We contemplate the truths He shows us. Indeed, we take time to chew on the things God points out to us.

And when you read the Bible, use your sanctified common sense! Don't just open the Scriptures and read without a plan. For you see, the Bible is like any other book; it has all kinds of forms of speech. You see poetry as poetry. You see prophecy as prophecy. You see precept as precept. You see the promise as a promise. And you see a proverb as a proverb.

For example, if you try to turn the proverbs into promises, you'll lose your religion. The proverbs are not promises, they are proverbs. What is a proverb? A proverb is a general principle, generally applied, which brings a general result. As you read each section of the Bible, use your mind and read wisely. Truly, you have the mind of Christ, and you need to use your mind as you study the Bible.

Some may ask how the Bible is to be interpreted—literally or figuratively. It is to be interpreted figuratively and literally all at the same time. For example, the Bible is full of symbols. In the book of the Revelation, the devil is symbolized as a dragon, a huge dragon. He has a tail so long that he sweeps a third of the stars from Heaven. But, the devil is also a reality—a real being who does real damage.

To assist you with your Bible study, I want to give you three practical and helpful questions to ask as you read:

- First, what did the passage mean back then? In the day when it was written, what did it mean?

- Second, what does the passage mean now? In today's terms, what do these verses mean for all of us?

- Third, what does the passage mean to me personally? How can I take and apply God's words?

After praying and pondering over the Scriptures, you will next want to preserve what you have read. Look at Psalm 119:11: "Your word I have hidden in my heart, that I might not sin against You." See also Psalm 119:16: "I will delight myself in Your statutes; I will not forget Your word." That means that preserve the Bible and hide it down in your heart. You can remember far more than you think you can remember.

Don't tell me you can't remember. You could not function if you couldn't remember things. You remember how to get to places like work, church, and the grocery store. You remember which pedal to press as you are driving; you know when to use the accelerator and when to use the brake. Truly, we function by using our memory. And memory comes with concentration. Your mind is a marvel, and you can remember far more than you think you can remember as you preserve the Word of God.

Let me give you an example. My wife has a love affair with little boxes, pretty little boxes. People will give her these boxes, many from other countries. The boxes are intricately carved and may have jewels on them. They are beautiful. But, what does she put on the insides of these pretty boxes? Rubber bands, gem clips, toothpicks, old breath mints, and so many other items are stored in these little boxes.

Your mind is like those boxes! You will fill it with all sorts of junk. Why not use your amazing mind for good? What a marvel

God gave you when God gave you a mind; and you can use it to meditate on the Word of God.

Another great picture of our minds is a garden. Have you ever noticed how much easier it is to grow weeds than flowers and vegetables? Well, Adam fell in the garden; his mind became a garden of weeds. For your mind to preserve the Word of God, you have got to cultivate your mind. You have to weed your mental garden.

In addition to preserving Scripture in your mind, you also must practice the Bible. Look at Psalm 119:1-4 to see what I mean: "Blessed are the undefiled in the way, who walk in the law of the LORD! Blessed are those who keep His testimonies, who seek Him with the whole heart! They also do no iniquity; they walk in His ways. You have commanded us to keep Your precepts diligently."

It's not enough to recite the promises without obeying the commandments of the Bible. If you want to learn more about the Word of God, you must obey what you do know to do. The more you obey, the more you will learn. You may feel like there is much of the Bible that you do not understand. Mark Twain is reported to have said, "It's not that part of the Bible that I don't understand that gives me so much trouble, it's the part I do understand."[40]

There may be mysteries and things you don't understand about the third toe on the left foot of some beast in Revelation. However, you can clearly understand commands in the Bible like Ephesians 4:32: "And be kind to one another, tenderhearted, forgiving one another, even as God in Christ forgave you." You and I can understand when the Bible gives us clear and plain commandments. And if you will begin to obey these commands, the Bible will become more real to you.

To assimilate the vitality of the Word of God, there is one more action we must take. We must proclaim the Word. Look in Psalm 119:13: "With my lips, I have declared all the judgments of Your mouth." Also, see Psalm 119:27: "Make me understand the way of Your precepts; so shall I meditate on Your wonderful works."

Let's consider a couple of other verses as well. Look at Psalm 119:46: "I will speak of Your testimonies also before kings and will not be ashamed." In Psalm 119:172, we read, "My tongue shall speak of Your word, for all Your commandments are righteousness."

To grow in the Lord, we need to give Scripture away. Let the Word of God be in your mouth, constantly in your mouth. Stow it in your heart, show it in your life, sow it in the world. The more of the Word of God you give away, the more of it will stick to you.

WE MUST APPROPRIATE THE VALUES OF THE WORD OF GOD

There's one final point I'd like to make in thinking about the Bible. You and I must appropriate the values of the word of God. We must allow God to transform us through what we read, study, ponder, and practice.

The Bible can be a source of victory for us as Christians. Consider the words of Psalm 119:45: "And I will walk at liberty, for I seek Your precepts." Scripture can also be a source of growth for us. Look at Psalm 119:32: "I will run the course of Your commandments, for You shall enlarge my heart." God's Word can empower you and give you the strength to grow. The Bible tells us in 1 Peter 2:2, "As newborn babes, desire the pure milk of the word, that you may grow thereby."

In like manner, the Bible is a source of joy for us as believers. Consider the words of Psalm 119:54: "Your statutes have been my songs in the house of my pilgrimage." In Psalm 119:111, we read, "Your testimonies I have taken as a heritage forever, for they are the rejoicing of my heart."

Jesus told His disciples in John 15:11, "These things I have spoken to you, that My joy may remain in you, and that your joy may be full."

The Bible is also a source of power and guidance. We read about the power of the Word in Psalm 119:28: "My soul melts from heaviness; strengthen me according to Your word." In Psalm 119:105, we find our source of guidance: "Your word is a lamp to my feet and a light to my path."

Do you want joy in your life? Power? Victory? Then you need to get into the Bible and appropriate what you read. You can appropriate Scripture, but you can only appropriate it after you assimilate it, and you can only assimilate it if you appreciate it. If you begin to make the Bible a regular part of your day, I promise you that God will transform your life.

For those of you who are not Christians, can I just give you the Bible in shorthand? The Bible addresses one problem, and that problem is sin. The Bible has one villain, and that villain is the devil. The Bible has one hero, and His name is Jesus. The Bible has one purpose, and that is the glory of God.

The Bible is a two-edged sword. If it doesn't cut to heal you, it will cut to slay you. You have a choice that comes right from the pages of the Word. You must choose what you will do with Jesus. John 3:16 tells us, "For God so loved the world that He gave His only begotten Son, that whoever believes in Him should not perish but have everlasting life."

Do you know Jesus? Why not invite Him to save you today? You can pray a simple prayer like this one: "Lord Jesus, come into my heart today. Forgive my sin and save me."

ENDNOTES

35. Author unknown.

36. Ward, Hannah, and Jennifer Wild. *Resources for Preaching and Worship -- Year B: Quotations, Meditations, Poetry, and Prayers*. Westminster John Knox Press, 2002.

37. Devotionals, Adrian Rogers' Daily. "Controlling Your Thought Life - Love Worth Finding - January 26." *Crosswalk.com*, Salem Web Network, 26 Jan. 2019, www.crosswalk.com/devotionals/loveworthfinding/love-worth-finding-january-26-2019.html.

38. Scottish Corner Research and Photos. "Preaching through the Bible in One Year PTB #10: Bible Consistency." *The Christian Mind*, 15 June 2019, sungrist.net/2019/06/15/preaching-thru-the-bible-in-one-year-ptb-10-bible-consistency/.

39. Timeless Truths Free Online Library | books, sheet music. "Jesus Loves Me." *Jesus Loves Me > Lyrics | Anna B. Warner*, library.timelesstruths.org/music/Jesus_Loves_Me/.

40. "Mark Twain Quotes." *BrainyQuote*, Xplore, www.brainyquote.com/quotes/mark_twain_153875.

THE PRINCIPLES OF PRAYER

MATTHEW 7:7-11

"God answers every prayer, in one way or another."
—*Adrian Rogers*

There is no substitute in the Christian life for prayer. Prayer is the believer's greatest privilege, and for most of us, it is also our greatest failure.

Other things may be good and fine in and of themselves, but they're not a substitute. Eloquence is not a substitute for prayer. Energy is not a substitute for prayer. Enthusiasm is not a substitute for prayer. Intellect is not a substitute for prayer. There is no substitute for prayer. Prayer, in my estimation, is the greatest untapped, unused force in the universe.

Think about it. People are always trying to tap into energy. Scientists have been looking at the energy of the ocean as the tides ebb and flow and the waves swell and think that somehow we could tap that energy. We seek after energy through the sun, through nuclear power, in coal, and other resources. However, the greatest unused, untapped energy in the world is prayer.

In Matthew 7:7-11, we are going to read the words of Jesus about prayer. Jesus said them clearly and plainly and we have no reason to doubt them, so we must believe them.

> Ask, and it will be given to you; seek, and you will find; knock, and it will be opened to you. For everyone who asks receives, and he who seeks finds, and to him who knocks it will be opened. Or what man is there among you who, if his son asks for bread, will give him a stone? Or if he asks for a fish, will he give him a serpent? If you then, being evil, know how to give good gifts to your children, how much more will your Father who is in heaven give good things to those who ask Him!

Consider with me these principles of prayer from the words of Jesus. Here are the reasons for prayer, the request in prayer, and the reward of prayer.

THE REASONS FOR PRAYER

Why does God want us to pray? Jesus taught very clearly that our heavenly Father knows the things you need before you ask. Isn't that true? He already knows what we need. And He is infinite love. So why should we have to pray? Why should we have to tell Him what we need? And why should we have to ask of Him what He already wants to give us because He loves us?

Have you ever thought about the mystery of prayer? Look at Matthew 6:7-8: "And when you pray, do not use vain repetitions as the heathen do. For they think that they will be heard for their many words. Therefore do not be like them. For your Father knows the things you have need of before you ask Him."

We learn some things from these verses. First, we do not pray to God to impress Him. You don't have to be a junior-size Shakespeare and pray in King James English. You don't have to be a poet and use flowery language.

Nor do you pray to inform God. In verse 8, we read, "Therefore do not be like them. For your Father knows the things you have need of before you ask Him." Your Father knows what things you need. So, why do we pray? We pray to invite God to work in our hearts and lives.

God wants us to love Him and take delight in Him. He wants us to fellowship with Him. God could run this universe without our prayers. But if He ran this universe without our prayers, you and I would not have the privilege of working with Him and fellowshipping with Him and being with Him as He administrates this great universe.

In the book of John, Jesus spoke of this relationship like branches attached to a grapevine. He is the vine, and we are the branches. Consider His words in John 15:4: "Abide in Me, and I in you. As the branch cannot bear fruit of itself, unless it abides in the vine, neither can you, unless you abide in Me." Prayer causes us to abide in Jesus.

Also, prayer is a way of God bonding us to Himself. Prayer causes us to dwell in Him and He in us until we have the same kind of a union that a branch has with a vine. We cannot do it without Him, and He will not do it without us.

Awhile back, a college called and asked me to speak on their campus. My schedule just wouldn't allow it. They offered to send a pilot to come and pick me up and fly me to the campus, to save time. When the pilot arrived, I got onto one of the smallest airplanes I've ever been on. While in the air, the pilot asked me if I'd like to try my hand at flying the plane. The pilot told me exactly what to do, and I flew the plane.

Yes, I flew. But, I could not have flown that plane without the pilot. He easily could have flown without me. But he gave me the privilege of flying that craft alongside him. And do you know it was a lot of fun? It was an experience I still remember. The experience caused us to bond and it forged a great friendship. I was thankful for his gracious spirit and the opportunity to fly with him.

After the experience, I thought to myself that prayer is a lot like me flying that plane. God allows us to cooperate with Him. Indeed, we have the thrill of helping God regulate this mighty universe. Prayer comes when we abide in Him and He abides in us.

There is also another facet of prayer. I call this the development factor. Did you know that prayer is one of the ways that we grow?

We are developed in prayer. In John 15:7, Jesus said, "If you abide in Me, and My words abide in you, you will ask what you desire, and it shall be done for you."

Sometimes we pray and the answer doesn't seem to come. This causes us to dig into the Bible and seek the face of God more. As we do this, we begin to grow in the grace and knowledge of our Lord and Savior Jesus Christ. Eventually, the answer to our prayers does come. The waiting and the abiding causes us to grow.

For example, suppose a boy has his eye on a particular girl that he'd like to date. When he asks her out the first time, she turns him down. So, he goes home and takes more care of his hygiene. He gets his hair cut and styled, cuts his fingernails, and puts on a clean shirt. Then, he asks her out again. And, again, she turns him down.

Not deterred by her refusals, that same boy decides it must be something else. He begins to work on his manners. Once again, he asks her out. This time, she says she will go. And none of this time was wasted. The whole time he's been asking her, he has been improving, he's been growing, and he's been getting more and more acceptable to her.

That's the way prayer is. We ask God for something and the answer doesn't come. And we ask again. When God doesn't answer, we begin to confess our sins and ask God what we need to work on. Maybe we are selfish? Maybe we don't have much faith? Maybe we aren't studying the Bible much? As we wait in prayer, we grow up, we develop, and we become more like Christ. Prayer is a form of character development.

Furthermore, prayer has a dependence factor about it. God never wants us to live independent of Him. Prayer causes us to lean hard upon the Lord Jesus Christ. In John 15:5, Jesus said, "I am the vine, you are the branches. He who abides in Me, and I in him, bears much fruit; for without Me you can do nothing."

It would be tragic if God were to run this universe and leave us out of it because we'd never know the delight of prayer. We would never know the growth and the development that comes through prayer. And we would never know that dependence upon God, that bonding that comes through prayer. So whether we understand the philosophy of prayer or not, we know that our Lord has invited us, and our Lord has commanded us to pray.

THE REQUEST IN PRAYER

Another facet of prayer is the request in prayer. Notice what Jesus says in Matthew 7:7: "Ask, and it will be given to you; seek, and you will find; knock, and it will be opened to you." He tells us first to ask. Did you know that the great problem in prayer is not unanswered prayer—it is unoffered prayer?

Look at James 4:2: "Yet you do not have because you do not ask." Jesus said we are to ask. Unoffered prayer is not merely a tragedy; it is a sin. We are commanded to pray and ask God. In Luke 18:1, we read, "Then He spoke a parable to them, that men always ought to pray and not lose heart." Jesus said to His disciples in Mark 14:38, "Watch and pray."

In Philippians 4:6 the Bible says, "Be anxious for nothing, but in everything by prayer and supplication, with thanksgiving, let your requests be made known to God." In everything! Prayer ought to be as normal, as natural as breathing. Paul said, "Pray about everything." If something concerns you, it concerns God too.

A good test of whether or not you ought to be participating in something or wanting something or attempting something is, can you pray about it? If you cannot pray about it, maybe you don't need to do it. And we don't have to divide life up into the secular and the sacred. We can pray about all things—the spiritual and the secular. You can pray when you are about to teach a Bible lesson and you can pray when you go fishing or go shopping.

For example, I was fishing down in Florida some years ago at Cape Canaveral on a sandbar with some buddies. We hadn't been fishing for long. I was using a mirror lure and a spin-casting outfit. A little distance from my friends, I was standing in water up to my knees. I could hear the other guys catching fish, but I hadn't caught one. So, I began to pray.

My prayer was pretty simple as I talked to God, "Lord, I'm not catching any fish. These other guys are catching fish. Lord, I've been working hard. This is the only time I've got to go fishing for a long time. And, Lord, I'm going to ask You to let me catch a speckled trout, not a little one but a big one."

After I prayed that prayer, I threw that mirror lure over into a deep hole there in the sandbar, and it sank to the bottom. And I twitched it and reeled it in a couple of times, and I saw something big and yellow coming out of the water. It was a mouth of a great big speckled trout. He was huge!

So I said, "Lord, let me catch another one." And I cast and I caught another fish right after I'd prayed. I'd been fishing for a long time without praying. After catching those fish, I wondered why I had waited so long to pray about my fishing.

Now, you may think that's a little frivolous. But I want to tell you something. None of us have any business doing anything that we can't pray about. I don't care what it is. If you can't pray about it, you've got no business doing it. If you can't ask God for it, you should not do it.

The Bible says in Philippians 4:6, "But in everything by prayer and supplication, with thanksgiving, let your requests be made known to God." That does mean everything. Can you think of anything too big for God to handle or anything too small for God to notice? Is anything too small for Him to care about?

What if you desire something that is not good and not positive? Pray about that as well. Tell God about your struggles and invite Him to change your heart. Our responsibility is the asking; God's responsibility is the giving. But He cannot do His responsibility unless we do ours. So our Lord tells us that we should ask.

Further, God says that we should seek. Not only should there be a desire; there needs to be discernment. What is discernment? When you are seeking discernment, it is as if you are on a quest. You're trying to find something. You're trying to discover something. Prayer helps us to find and discover wisely.

How do we know that we are seeking the purpose of God? How to we pray in the will of God? Look at James 4:3: "You ask and do not receive, because you ask amiss, that you may spend it on your pleasures." If you're asking for the wrong thing, God's not going to bless you. God's not going to give it to you.

Maybe it might be that you're selfish in your motivation. I can ask for personal needs, but I can't ask for selfish needs. It may be just God Himself that He wants me to seek. Maybe before God gives me what He wants, He wants me to want Him more than I want the thing I'm asking for.

In James 4:8, God reminds us, "Draw near to God and He will draw near to you. Cleanse your hands, you sinners; and purify your hearts, you double-minded." It may be that God wants me just to draw nigh to Him and to seek Him, to get away from my frivolous, half-hearted prayers. God does business with those that mean business.

Also, it could be that God wants me to seek the power of God that comes through purity, for He goes on to say in James 5:16, "Confess your trespasses to one another, and pray for one another, that you may be healed. The effective, fervent prayer of a righteous man avails much." As we fervently seek the Lord, we can ask Him what He wants us to pray, seek, and find.

Another facet of our prayer requests is determination. We ask, we seek, and we knock. What do you knock on? You knock on a closed door. When you pray, you keep on praying until that door opens. There are barriers that we have to overcome when we pray. And the verb *knock* means to keep on knocking.

Sometimes God's answers are direct. You ask God for something and He gives it to you immediately. We've all had that to happen to us. But sometimes God's answers are different. We ask for one thing, and He gives us something else. Sometimes God's answers are denied. We ask for something and God doesn't give it to us. At other times, we ask, and God's answers are delayed. This is when we have to knock, and we have to keep on knocking.

This is a hard prayer concept to understand. To keep knocking without getting an answer is a challenging thing to do. In Luke 11:1, the disciples asked the Lord to teach them to pray. In verses 5-8, Jesus told them a story.

And He said to them, "Which of you shall have a friend, and go to him at midnight and say to him, 'Friend, lend me three loaves; for a friend of mine has come to me on his journey, and I have nothing to set before him'; and he will answer from within and say, 'Do not trouble me; the door is now shut, and my children are with me in bed; I cannot rise and give to you'? I say to you, though he will not rise and give to him because he is his friend, yet because of his persistence he will rise and give him as many as he needs."

Now, do you get the picture? Here's a man who is knocking on his neighbor's door. He asks his neighbor for extra food to feed his houseguest. But the neighbor tries to get him to leave using his children as an excuse. Yes, the knocking man is persistent and continues to knock. Eventually, the neighbor gets up and helps him because of his urgency and persistence. Jesus encourages us to do the same in our prayer lives. Keep knocking. Be persistent. Don't stop praying!

We are to ask with desire. Also, we are to seek discernment. And, finally, we are to knock with determination. Whether you understand it or not, you've got to knock on heaven's door, and you have to keep on knocking sometimes to get those prayers answered.

Consider another great Bible example in Luke 18.

Then He spoke a parable to them, that men always ought to pray and not lose heart, saying: "There was in a certain city a judge who did not fear God nor regard man. Now there was a widow in that city; and she came to him, saying, 'Get justice for me from my adversary.' And he would not for a while; but afterward, he said within himself, 'Though I do not fear God nor regard man, yet because this widow troubles me I will avenge her, lest by her continual coming she weary me.'" Then the Lord said, "Hear what the unjust judge said. And shall God not avenge His own elect who cry out day and night to Him, though He bears long with them?

Jesus said we are to keep on knocking until we get an answer. In Isaiah 30:18, we read, "Therefore the LORD will wait, that He may be gracious to you; and therefore He will be exalted, that He may

THE PRINCIPLES OF PRAYER

have mercy on you. For the LORD is a God of justice; blessed are all those who wait for Him."

Let me give you another example of this same kind of determination. Look in Matthew 15:21-28 to the story of Jesus and the faith of the Syrophoenician woman.

> Then Jesus went out from there and departed to the region of Tyre and Sidon. And behold, a woman of Canaan came from that region and cried out to Him, saying, "Have mercy on me, O Lord, Son of David! My daughter is severely demon-possessed." But He answered her not a word. And His disciples came and urged Him, saying, "Send her away, for she cries out after us." But He answered and said, "I was not sent except to the lost sheep of the house of Israel." Then she came and worshiped Him, saying, "Lord, help me!" But He answered and said, "It is not good to take the children's bread and throw it to the little dogs." And she said, "Yes, Lord, yet even the little dogs eat the crumbs which fall from their masters' table." Then Jesus answered and said to her, "O woman, great is your faith! Let it be to you as you desire." And her daughter was healed from that very hour.

This woman came and said to Jesus asking for mercy for her demon-possessed daughter. Jesus refused her and tried to send her away. But, she was relentless. She appealed to Jesus, and Jesus had compassion on her and healed her daughter.

Be certain, Jesus is not saying God is an unjust judge. And He is not comparing God to a selfish neighbor. God is not a respecter of persons. These stories are to teach us to press on and to press through in prayer. We need to ask. And, many times, we have not because we ask not.

Let me share another example of persevering in prayer. This one is found in 1 Kings 18:41-45. In this story, Elijah has prayed because it has not rained in several years. God tells Elijah that it is going to rain.

> And Elijah went up to the top of Carmel; then he bowed
> down on the ground, and put his face between his knees,
> and said to his servant, "Go up now, look toward the
> sea." So he went up and looked, and said, "There is
> nothing." And seven times he said, "Go again." Then
> it came to pass the seventh time, that he said, "There
> is a cloud, as small as a man's hand, rising out of the
> sea!" So he said, "Go up, say to Ahab, 'Prepare your
> chariot, and go down before the rain stops you.'" Now
> it happened in the meantime that the sky became black
> with clouds and wind, and there was a heavy rain.

God has told Elijah that it is going to rain. But, he prays again and again for the rain to come. Finally, on the seventh prayer, a little cloud showed up in the sky. It looked like it was the size of a man's hand. Why didn't God send the rain the first time? I don't know, but He didn't do it.

God had promised to send the rain. But Elijah had to pray seven times. He had to ask God for the rain seven different times. There's a great lesson in this story: God's delays are not God's denials. God has the right time. And He is always right.

Do you remember that Jesus also had to knock on heaven's door in prayer? You would think Jesus' prayers would be automatically answered, but that was not always the case. Consider the example found in Matthew 26:44: "So He left them, went away again, and prayed the third time, saying the same words." Think about these words. Jesus prayed a third time the very same words. There is a truth here, a mystery we may never understand. We are to keep knocking, over and over again, in prayer.

Is there a time when we can stop knocking? A time when we quit seeking and asking? When the door opens, you can stop knocking. Or, when you have the assurance in your heart that it's time to stop praying about something, you can stop.

Paul, the mighty apostle, had a situation like this. We read that he prayed three times for God to take something away. After the third time, he sensed that God was telling him, "No." It was time to stop praying about this burden. Look at what he writes in 2 Corinthians 12:8-9.

Concerning this thing, I pleaded with the Lord three times that it might depart from me. And He said to me, "My grace is sufficient for you, for My strength is made perfect in weakness." Therefore most gladly I will rather boast in my infirmities, that the power of Christ may rest upon me.

When do you stop praying about something? When the door opens, and you have what you ask. Or when you know in your heart that it is time to stop asking. You have the peace to accept what you cannot change. God gives you the grace to move on and stop knocking, asking, and seeking.

About six years ago, God told me that He heard a prayer from me. I'd been knocking and even kicking at the door. I prayed again and again and again and again. God assured me He had heard my prayer, and that it was time to stop asking. In addition, He gave me the peace in my heart to stop asking for this thing.

God answers every prayer, in one way or another. Sometimes, the answer is, "Yes." Have you ever asked God for something and He just gave it to you just like you asked Him for it? Don't you love that? I think we all do. We love unmistakable answers to prayer. Sometimes the answer is, "Yes."

However, sometimes the answer is, "No." We ask for the wrong things or we ask with the wrong motives. And God doesn't send us what we ask for.

At other times, the answer is, "Wait." God may send us what we are asking for, but we are going to have to wait for it. We need some character development, and the timing is not yet right. We will need to wait for the answer to come.

There's one other answer to prayer that we must consider. Sometimes God doesn't give us what we ask for because He wants to give us something better. He has a plan that is, "exceedingly abundantly above all that we ask or think" (Ephesians 3:20).

THE REWARD OF PRAYER

There is one more facet of prayer to consider. This is the reward of prayer.

For everyone who asks receives, and he who seeks finds, and to him who knocks it will be opened. Or what man is there among you who, if his son asks for bread, will give him a stone? Or if he asks for a fish, will he give him a serpent? If you then, being evil, know how to give good gifts to your children, how much more will your Father who is in heaven give good things to those who ask Him! (Matthew 7:8-11)

Why can we be so assured that God's going to answer our prayers? Because God is good. Notice the logic of Jesus. If evil men will take care of their children, how much more shall a good God answer the prayers of His children?

And not only is God good, but God is wise. God is not going to give you something that would harm you. God is not going to give you stones if we ask for bread. He's not going to give us snakes when we ask for fish. God is all-wise, and He is all-love! So let's remember to come to God in prayer, to keep on praying and to keep on asking.

LEARNING TO SHARE JESUS

PSALM 126:5-6

"If you are not endeavoring to share your faith, in my humble but accurate opinion, you're not right with God."
—Adrian Rogers

H ave you ever shared your faith in Jesus with another person? Maybe given your testimony? That's what we are going to talk about today. I pray that God will use the message in this chapter to plant in your heart a desire to share your faith.

When I gave my heart to Jesus Christ as a teenager, one of the ways I knew my decision was real is that I had a deep desire to share what happened to me with my brother, my sister, and my friends. I wanted them to know the Jesus that I had met. May I ask you today, do you have a desire to give your faith away? If not, then it's not much of a faith. Love worth finding is also love worth sharing.

Although I'm grateful for people who sing in the choir, play instruments, work in the nursery, give to the poor, and do all sorts of other acts of service. If you are not endeavoring to share your faith, in my humble but accurate opinion, you're not right with God. No matter how eloquently you preach, no matter how beautifully you sing, no matter how generously you give, no matter how faithfully you attend, and no matter how circumspectly you walk, there is no substitute for sharing your faith with other people.

Look at Psalm 126:5-6: "Those who sow in tears shall reap in joy. He who continually goes forth weeping, bearing seed for sowing, shall doubtless come again with rejoicing, bringing his sheaves with him." The Bible tells us that as we sow and reap, we will understand the secret of sharing our faith.

Check out Proverbs 11:30: "The fruit of the righteous is a tree of life, and he who wins souls is wise." Do you consider yourself to be a wise person? Why is it so wise to bring a soul to Jesus Christ, to teach somebody to know and love the Lord Jesus Christ?

One of the reasons soul winning is wise is because of the value of a soul to Almighty God. Remember what Jesus said in Mark 8:36-37? "For what will it profit a man if he gains the whole world, and loses his own soul? Or what will a man give in exchange for his soul?" A soul is so incredibly valuable that Jesus taught that one soul is worth more than the whole world. So, if you won just one soul to Jesus Christ, that is amazing!

Why is a soul so valuable? First of all, a soul is of value because of its desirability. Did you know that the devil desires your soul at the same time God desires your soul? How can we tell whether a thing is desirable or not? By the price someone will pay for it. Jesus, with His precious blood on the cross, died that a soul might be redeemed. Any appraiser will tell you the value of a piece of property is this: what someone else will pay for it.

An evangelist friend of mine was wasting his life. Lost and away from God, he was throwing his life away. Someone told him how much God loved him and how much value he had to God. He gave his heart to Christ and began serving Him when he realized how desirable his soul was to God. Indeed, a soul is desirable. Jesus paid His rich, red, royal blood for a soul.

Not only is a soul desirable, but a soul is also durable. A soul will last for all eternity. Your soul will go on endless, dateless, timeless, measureless, and throughout all eternity. When the stars have splintered and faded, your soul will be in existence somewhere. That's the value of a soul.

Jesus spoke of those in hell and talked about the torment they face forever and ever. Look at Luke 16:23 where Jesus spoke of this torment: "And being in torments in Hades, he lifted up his eyes and saw Abraham afar off, and Lazarus in his bosom." The same is true of heaven. Some souls will spend an eternity in heaven. Throughout all the endless ages, a soul will be in existence, either in Heaven or in Hell.

In addition to these things, a soul also contains an incredible possibility. No man or woman is worthless. Christ died for all of us. Think of the woman at the well and how Jesus transformed her from living in sin to living like a saint. In the same vein, we think of Rahab the harlot, who is now saved and in Heaven, shining as a bright star in the Savior's crown. Hebrews 11:31 tells us, "By faith the harlot Rahab did not perish with those who did not believe when she had received the spies with peace."

You and I have the choice to be one of three people. We can be the person we are right now. Or we can be the person who lives for evil and fails to follow God. Or, we can be the person who chooses to be made like into the likeness of our Lord and Savior Jesus Christ. Which person will you choose to be?

Truly, when you win souls, you're wise because of the value of a soul. And when you win souls, you're wise because of the command of the Savior. Jesus has commanded us to make disciples. This is not a suggestion or a request. The Christian who does not share his faith is guilty of high treason against his God. In Matthew 28:19, Jesus instructed us to, "Go therefore and make disciples of all the nations, baptizing them in the name of the Father and of the Son and the Holy Spirit."

Also, Jesus said in Matthew 4:19, "Follow Me, and I will make you fishers of men." If you're not fishing for men, by what right of logic do you have to say that you're following Jesus? You're not following Christ. You're not abiding in Christ. In John 15:5, Jesus said, "I am the vine, you are the branches. He who abides in Me, and I in him, bears much fruit; for without Me you can do nothing."

Can I ask you a couple of honest questions? Are you bearing fruit? Are people coming to know the Lord Jesus Christ through your life? If not, then you're not abiding in Christ. Do you love Jesus? Jesus said, "If you love Me, keep My commandments" (John 14:15). Are you keeping His commandments? What right do you have to say that you love the Lord Jesus if you're not obeying His chief commandment to share your faith?

Why is winning souls so wise? Because of the value of a soul, because of the command of Christ, and because of the reward of the soul winner. There is great reward in sharing Christ with others.

To share your faith in Jesus Christ and to see your brother, your sister, your father, your mother, your friend, your neighbor, your teammate, your school mate, or whoever come to Christ brings one of the greatest rewards that life can ever know. What joy it is to bring people to Jesus Christ!

You see, many of us are committed to something. What are you committed to? What matters to you? And what is going to matter for all eternity?

For example, if you are a football fan, you will remember Don Shula, who was one of the great football coaches of all time. For years, Shula coached for the Miami Dolphins. The story is told that he and his wife tried to sneak away for a few days of vacation. They went to New Hampshire, thinking that no one would know them way up there.

When they got off the airplane and checked into a hotel, they decided to take in a movie. It was a small town, and they thought it might be fun to catch a show. Unexpectedly, as they walked into the theatre, people began to applaud. Shula thought, "I can't even go to a movie in this little town without people knowing me."

Funny thing though, the clapping wasn't about Shula's coaching fame. Instead, another moviegoer leaned over to Coach Shula and said, "We are sure glad to see you. The manager of the movie theatre just said that he wasn't going to start the movie until two more people came in. You two walked in, and now we get to watch the show. Thank you!"

Fame is fleeting. Notoriety is short-lived. But to win souls is to invest in something that will last for all of eternity. To share your faith is to make a difference in someone else's life forever. For this reason, let's consider four factors that will help you to better share your faith.

YOU MUST BE COMMITTED TO SHARE YOUR FAITH

To learn to share your faith, you must be committed. Look again with me at Psalm 126:5-6: "Those who sow in tears shall reap in joy. He who continually goes forth weeping, bearing seed for sowing, shall doubtless come again with rejoicing, bringing his sheaves with him." You must be intentional about winning souls. It's not an easy thing to do. But it is something we *must* do.

Some people tell me they just try to live a good life so others will want to be saved. However, people are not saved by your life; they are saved by Jesus' death. And if you live a good life without letting people know why you live that good life, you're taking praise under false pretenses. Anything good about you is Jesus Christ in you, and you have to share that. Truly, you will never be a soul winner until you start telling others about Jesus.

Our Lord tells us to go and tell. In Mark 16:15, we read, "And He said to them, 'Go into all the world and preach the gospel to every creature.'" In the Greek language, *to go* means as you go or as you are going.

Certainly, it's a joy to be a part of a church and a community of believers. It's so sweet to gather with our friends and family. But what might happen if all of us went out of these communities and shared Christ with those around us? How might our world improve and change if believers started to boldly share their faith? People need a Savior. And, we have to be committed to sharing our faith.

Some people tell themselves they are trying to avoid the world because they desire to live holy lives—separate from the world. You can be separate and holy, but you also need to understand that separation is not isolation. Jesus was a friend of sinners. That's why they crucified Him.

We read in Luke 15:2, "And the Pharisees and scribes complained, saying, 'This Man receives sinners and eats with them.'"

Thank God that Jesus loves sinners. If He didn't, none of us would be saved.

I heard of a little boy who didn't use good English. He told his mother, "I ain't going."

His mother corrected him and said, "Now, son, it is not 'I ain't going.' It's 'I am not going.' 'She is not going.' 'He is not going.' Do you understand that?"

He said, "Yeah, it looks like ain't nobody going."

When I look at the church, I feel the same way. Why do we do so little with so much? Have you ever thought about it? The unsaved are not commanded to go to church. We think that if we build beautiful buildings and offer wonderful programs, people should stream in the doors of our churches. However, nothing in Scripture tells unsaved people to go to church.

However, I can find Scripture after Scripture after Scripture that tells the church to go to the unsaved. It's our job to go to them, not to get them to come to us. If you've ever been hunting, you know that the deer are not supposed to come to the cabin; you have to go hunt for the deer. Similarly, we are to go out into the highways and the hedges and compel lost people to come in.

Most believers want to go to church. It's a joy to be with our brothers and sisters. But, lost people don't have any desire to come to church. If they come, it is because they have been lovingly invited and entreated by someone who cares about them. Typically, if we graciously invite someone to church, they will come.

YOU MUST BE CONCERNED WHEN YOU SHARE YOUR FAITH

Not only must we be committed to sharing our faith, but we must be concerned when we do share. Look again at Psalm 126:5: "Those who sow in tears shall reap in joy." It's amazing that we, in the church, have such a lack of tears for the lost. We are not passionate about telling people about Jesus.

Can I ask you a sincere question? Do the things that break the heart of Jesus break yours? Jesus wept over Jerusalem in Luke 19:41-44. What about you? Are you afraid of tears? Did you know that the Apostle Paul wept over the lost? In Acts 20:31, Paul wrote, "Therefore watch, and remember that for three years I did not cease to warn every one night and day with tears."

With tears! When's the last time you shed a tear over some soul that's mortgaged to the devil? Do you weep over the plight of the unsaved, the lost, the doomed, the damned, on their road to hell, with no hope? In Jeremiah 9:1, the prophet Jeremiah wept over his people, "Oh, that my head were waters, and my eyes a fountain of tears, that I might weep day and night for the slain of the daughter of my people!"

Do you know what's wrong with many churches today? There's no brokenness. There's no heartache, no tears. Bible study classes meet without being concerned about the lost. Choirs practice and sing without any concern for the lost. However, we need to see every person as a potential brother or sister.

Years ago, I read about an episode that happened in Florida near Tampa. There was a high-powered boat going under a bridge when it hit a bridge abutment. The man in the boat was thrown out of the boat and knocked unconscious. It looked like he had drowned. The men that had fished him out of the water were giving him mouth to mouth resuscitation.

Soon after, a concerned motorist stopped his car to watch. He saw the sinking boat and the heroics going on. He shook his head, acknowledging that it was a sad situation. But then something changed as he walked over closer. This motorist noticed that the drowning man was his brother. His whole demeanor changed as rushed over to the scene and begin trying to help.

What had changed? What had transformed the motorist? His concern went from an intellectual interest in a situation to an emotional one. He wasn't just an onlooker to a tragedy; he was personally vested in what was taking place.

In our lives, we need to see every person as an individual who needs a Savior. We don't just need to see lost people intellectually; we need to also see them emotionally. Indeed, we need to see them as God sees them—with a broken heart. If you don't have a broken heart for the unsaved, I suggest that you get alone with God and invite Him to give you compassion for the lost. Jesus was moved with compassion for the multitudes, as we read in Matthew 9:36.

Today, we are "A dry-eyed church in a hell-bent world."[41] We are not concerned about the lost or souls coming to Jesus. But many of us have brothers and sisters and fathers and mothers and neighbors who, if they die in their state today, will go to hell. We claim to have the answer, and we must be willing to share our faith with compassion and love.

YOU MUST BE CONSISTENT TO SHARE YOUR FAITH

To share Christ with others, we must also be consistent as we share. In Psalm 126:5-6, the Scripture reads, "Those who sow in tears shall reap in joy. He who continually goes forth weeping, bearing seed for sowing, shall doubtless come again with rejoicing, bringing his sheaves with him." The idea of bearing precious seed is just scattering the seed everywhere you go.

What is the seed? The seed is the Word of God. Jesus, in the parable of the sower, said the seed is the Word. First Peter 1:23 tells us, "Having been born again, not of corruptible seed but incorruptible, through the word of God which lives and abides forever." We have the precious Word of God. Everywhere we go, we need to be consistent in sharing the seed because the seed has power.

Years ago, I read about a woman who thought that she would somehow protect her body from decay when she died. Because she was a rich woman, she made plans with her lawyer to have her body buried in a huge concrete vault. Steel bands were to be constructed all around the vault. And, on the outside of this vault, she wanted these words to be inscribed, *"Sealed for Eternity."*

Guess what happened to that vault? A hairline fracture began to form, and the seeds fell into these little cracks. Eventually, the seeds sprouted and began to grow. As the pressure of the roots mounted, the vault cracked wide open. This woman who thought her body was sealed for all eternity was uprooted by one little seed.

God's Word is like that little seed. It is so powerful that it can crack open even the hardest heart. Never diminish the power of the Word of God. The Bible is incredibly powerful. And, when you share the words of Scripture with a lost person, God uses the seed of His Word to touch their heart.

Do you want a harvest? Well, you have to sow to have a harvest. The Bible says whatever we sow, we'll reap. You sow the Word of God. You just share what Jesus Christ has done for you.

A preacher went to the local Wal-Mart to buy some fishing tackle. When he got to the fishing section of the store, he asked the clerk for a suggestion on the best lure for catching bass. A total stranger heard him ask the question and came racing over to give the preacher all sorts of suggestions. Even after the preacher had found what he needed and walked toward the register to pay, that man was still following him and telling him all sorts of facts about bass, hooks, lures, and boats.

It was obvious that this man loved fishing. He was a man who greatly enjoyed sharing his experiences and expertise. This man was a great witness for fishing. Similarly, we are to be witnesses to our faith. However, we are only called to be witnesses, not lawyers or judges. Our job is to tell what we have seen and heard. We share what Christ has done in our lives. That is it.

YOU MUST BE CONFIDENT TO SHARE YOUR FAITH

There's one final facet to witnessing. To be a witness, we must be confident in sharing our faith. Look again at Psalm 126:5-6: "Those who sow in tears shall reap in joy. He who continually goes forth weeping, bearing seed for sowing, shall doubtless come again with rejoicing, bringing his sheaves with him."

Truthfully, not everyone you witness to is going to be saved. Most of the people we share Christ with will not accept Him. However, some will get saved. Some will listen and want the Jesus you tell them about.

When a sower goes out to sow, not all of the seed that he sows sprouts. Farmers must sow lavishly, and so must we. Do you remember the parable there in Mark 4? Some seed fell by the wayside, and the birds came and got it. Some seed fell on stony ground and it sprang up and then withered. A few seeds fell among the thorns and the thorns choked them out. But some seed fell on good soil and flourished.

You don't know who's going to get saved. So you keep sharing your faith. You scatter the seed. Then, God gives the increase, not you. Your job is to scatter the seed. Some will get saved, others will not. Sometimes the most unlikely people will receive the seed that you scatter. You just never know, and so you sow.

A while back I got a letter from a man I hadn't seen in a long time. This is what his letter said:

> Forgive me for not writing to you sooner, but I want to tell you what happened to me. Years ago, when you were a pastor in Merritt Island, Florida, I was a long-haired, hippy, surfer. I had a surfboard, going down the street on a hot day, and you stopped and picked me up in your car. During the drive, you shared Jesus Christ with me. I was trying to act cool and act like I was paying no attention to you. I kind of pretended to brush you off. But you witnessed to me. You shared Jesus Christ with me, and you prayed with me and let me out of the car. I never got your witness out of my heart until I gave my heart to Jesus Christ, and God has saved me. And now I'm a preacher of the Gospel of our Lord and Savior Jesus Christ.

Honestly, I had to think hard to even remember the incident after I got the letter because I was just throwing out the seed. I had forgotten all about this man. But God hadn't. If you'll go and weep and pray and share and give, and always do it consistently, you're going to have the greatest joy in the world. You will be able to take these souls that you've reached, these sheaves, and lay them at Jesus' feet.

You may think that witnessing won't work. But I can assure you that God blesses a faithful witness. He blesses the seed that we consistently sow in the lives of others. Sometimes it takes a long time for your crop to harvest and come in. But God is faithful.

CONCLUSION

Some years ago, there was a man over which I got a great burden. He was in the medical field, a doctor, and he was a devout Jew. We had a good relationship, and he would sometimes watch me preach on television. When I'd see him out and about, he'd say, "You are a *good talker*."

Very slowly, I began to share Jesus with this dear man. We became friends and went to many college football games together. He had season tickets with wonderful seats, and he'd take me with him to some of the games. With each game, I became bolder and bolder in sharing Christ with him.

Finally, he told me that I was talking about Jesus with him a great deal. He asked if we could spend time together without talking about Jesus and still be friends. I reluctantly agreed to his request.

Years passed and I continued to pray for this man. One day, he had a serious heart attack. When I went to see him at the hospital, he wanted to talk with me about Heaven. I told him that he might be only a heartbeat away from Heaven. This startled him, and he asked me to tell him more. So I did. And, that Jewish doctor prayed and asked Christ into his heart. After years of sharing my faith with him, he finally was open.

I went home from the hospital that night elated. Indeed, I was so thrilled that God gave me the privilege to bring just one soul to Jesus Christ. The words to Psalm 126:5-6 came to mind: "Those who sow in tears shall reap in joy. He who continually goes forth weeping, bearing seed for sowing, shall doubtless come again with rejoicing, bringing his sheaves with him."

I can honestly tell you there is no greater joy than bringing a soul to Jesus Christ. However, most of us have to get jump-started now and then. It's so easy to go to church, to study our Bible, to have our devotions, and live our lives without ever sharing our faith.

All of the soul winning you and I will ever do will happen in this world. There will be no soul winning in Heaven. And one of these days, we will meet our Savior and have to answer for how we spent our days. The words to an old hymn come to mind:

Must I go, and empty-handed,
Thus my dear Redeemer meet?
Not one day of service give Him,
Lay no trophy at His feet?

Must I go, and empty-handed?
Must I meet my Savior so?
Not one soul with which to greet Him:
Must I empty-handed go?[42]

Maybe you could pray this prayer:

Lord, would you give me a burden for the unsaved? And, would you lay a particular person on my heart to begin to pray for? Would you lead me to someone who needs You? And, would you give me the courage to share my faith with them when the opportunity arises?

ENDNOTES

41. *A New Thing!*, www.bmcog.org/sermons/oct/2011/new_aud.html.
42. "Hymn: Must I Go, and Empty-Handed." *Hymnalnet RSS*, www.hymnal.net/en/hymn/h/930.

THE SOUL WINNER'S SIX MIGHTY MOTIVATIONS

2 CORINTHIANS 5

"Truthfully, if you are not attempting to bring souls to Christ, you are not pleasing God."
—*Adrian Rogers*

What motivates you? Did you know that your achievement in life will be primarily impacted and impelled by your motivations? What motivates you and drives you will cause you to become the person you ultimately end up becoming.

There was a story I heard of a middle school boy who was walking through the woods. He wasn't moving very fast until he heard a growl. When he looked behind him, he saw a huge grizzly bear. Immediately, he began to run like crazy through those woods. But as he ran, he could find no place to hide.

Then, he saw a tree with some lower hanging branches. The closest limb seemed to be about 15 feet in the air. He psyched himself up to jump as high as he could. When he felt the warm, moist breath of the bear on his neck, he prayed and jumped with all of his might. He missed the limb as he went up, but he caught it on the way down. That's motivation.

Today, let's think about motivation—great motivation to become a soul winner. Indeed, we've been praying for revival, for a sweeping revival. We are asking God to lead souls to Himself. And, part of this revival will include us winning souls to Christ.

The mightiest soul winner that I've known or read about is the Apostle Paul. In 2 Corinthians 5, we discover what motivated Paul, what drove him, and what made him the greatest missionary the world has ever known. For this reason, we can learn from his example.

If you've never been a soul winner, this is your chance to begin. And, if you are a soul winner, I believe you will be greatly blessed and encouraged as we study. Notice with me six motivations of a soul winner that we learn from the Apostle Paul.

THE SOUL WINNER'S COMPULSION

First, let's see the soul winner's compulsion. Paul had a compelling motive that drove him. What was Paul's compulsion? Look at 2 Corinthians 5:9: "Therefore we make it our aim, whether present or absent, to be well-pleasing to Him." This Scripture doesn't mean that we work our way to Heaven. Instead, Paul is encouraging us to make it our aim to be pleasing to God.

Truthfully, if you are not attempting to bring souls to Christ, you are not pleasing God. It doesn't matter how much money you give, how faithfully you go to church, or how circumspectly you walk. If you are not telling others about Jesus, you are not pleasing your heavenly Father. No matter who you please, if you displease God, you are a failure. The sweetest way to please God is to win souls. That should be your compulsion.

Author Andrew Murray wrote, "There are two classes of Christians: soul winners and backsliders."[43] You are either one or the other. Paul believed this. And he worked hard, preached hard, traveled, ministered, shared the Gospel, and wrote letters to churches because he was compelled to please God.

THE SOUL WINNER'S COMPENSATION

There's a second motivation for soul winning. This is the soul winner's compensation. Look at 2 Corinthians 5:10: "For we must all appear before the judgment seat of Christ, that each one may receive the things done in the body, according to what he has done, whether good or bad." There is a day coming when we will be compensated. The Bible calls that the *Judgment Seat of Christ.*

This compensation day is not the same as the Great White Throne Judgment where the unsaved will appear. The word for *judgment seat* in 2 Corinthians 5:10 is the Greek word *bema.* The *bema seat* in Bible days was a raised platform in the middle of the Olympic field. When runners would win a race, they would climb up onto the bema seat to get their reward. If they didn't win, they weren't invited to stand on the stage. No reward was given to them.

Winners would have a laurel placed on their heads which would eventually wilt and fade away. But one day, when we stand before Christ, we will have the chance to receive rewards that will never fade away. Those who win souls to Christ will be richly rewarded at the judgment seat. They will be sweetly compensated.

What will this look like? What is our compensation going to be? Look at 1 Corinthians 9:24-26.

> Do you not know that those who run in a race all run, but one receives the prize? Run in such a way that you may obtain it. And everyone who competes for the prize is temperate in all things. Now they do it to obtain a perishable crown, but we for an imperishable crown. Therefore I run thus: not with uncertainty. Thus I fight not as one who beats the air.

Paul advises us that if we are going to run in a race, we run to win. If you want to get the crown, you've got to train yourself. You have got to discipline yourself. You have to run with all of your might. And when you box, it's not shadow boxing, as one who is beating the air. This is a fight and it is a real fight. Do you realize that one of these days you're going to face the Lord and receive a crown if you're a soul winner?

Years ago, I played football. I was the captain of a championship team. Our team was awarded a small gold football which I gave to my wife (then girlfriend). We also wore letters on our jackets that identified us as players on our high school team. Along the way, I was blessed to receive some trophies.

For years, we kept all of those trophies and that gold football in our home. But, one night some thieves broke in and stole the golden football. I have no idea where it is now. And my letterman jacket was eaten by the moths long ago. Who knows where all those trophies are today? As a matter of fact, all of those awards, trophies, and accolades are long gone.

However, may I tell you something amazing? All of those souls that I've shared Jesus with and won to Christ still exist. When you win souls to Jesus Christ, you don't receive a corruptible crown. You receive a crown that will not fade away.

What is this Judgment Seat of Christ? For some, it's going to be a place of reward. For others, it's going to be a place of regret.

> For no other foundation can anyone lay than that which is laid, which is Jesus Christ. Now if anyone builds on this foundation with gold, silver, precious stones, wood, hay, straw, each one's work will become clear; for the Day will declare it, because it will be revealed by fire; and the fire will test each one's work, of what sort it is. If anyone's work which he has built on it endures, he will receive a reward. If anyone's work is burned, he will suffer loss; but he himself will be saved, yet so as through fire. (1 Corinthians 3:11-15)

What is this passage telling us? There will be no rewards for Sunday morning benchwarmers in Heaven. There is a judgment for all believers. Every mother's child is going to come to the Judgment Seat of Christ, the *bema* if you've been saved. Truly, we will stand before God and give account for the way we have lived.

One of these days you're going to see a replay of that old television program, "This Is Your Life." You will stand before the Lord and be reviewed. If you are a soul winner, your life will be gold and silver and precious stones. If you're not a soul winner, your life will be wood, hay, and stubble. Gold and silver and precious stones can't burn; they've already been through the fire. Wood, hay, and stubble will be consumed by the fire. Without a doubt, your life will be revealed and tested by fire.

So, what's it going to be? I want you to imagine yourself right now standing before the Judgment Seat of Christ. Are you going to be satisfied? There will be rewards for some. Will you be one of them?

Some people don't believe in rewards in Heaven. God does. Look at Revelation 22:12: "And behold, I am coming quickly, and My reward is with Me, to give to every one according to his work." See also 1 Corinthians 3:8: "Now he who plants and he who waters are one, and each one will receive his own reward according to his own labor."

In Matthew 6:20, Jesus said, "But lay up for yourselves treasures in heaven, where neither moth nor rust destroys and where thieves do not break in and steal." Don't get the idea that everybody's going to be the same in Heaven. They're not. We will not all have the same treasures or rewards. The Judgment Seat of Christ that Paul is talking about here in 2 Corinthians 5 is all about rewards.

Some Christians are sadly going to get to Heaven saved but singed. In other words, some will enter Heaven with the hems of their clothes smoking. After they go through the flames, there will nothing left but their souls. Everything they lived for will be burned up in the fire.

Before you know it, you will be standing before the Judgment Seat of Christ and receive the things done in your body, whether these be good or evil. There's not going to be any soul winning in Heaven. All the soul winning you're ever going to do for all eternity you must do now. How sad it will be to go to Heaven and not have won souls or brought souls to Jesus. Don't you want to take somebody to Heaven with you?

Years ago, I went to visit a man who spent his entire life working for the Southern Baptist Convention. On his deathbed, he called and asked me to come and talk to him. I'll never forget what he said to me. He said, "Pastor, I am saved, and I'm going to Heaven. I am not afraid to die. But, I am ashamed to die because I've not been a soul winner. I've never led anyone to Christ."

Can you imagine facing the Lord Jesus Christ without ever trying to bring a soul to Christ? Can you imagine going empty-handed to Heaven? Some people don't care as long as they make it to Heaven. They will just barely skirt into the pearly gates, but they will do so without taking thought of any other souls. That's not what I want. I pray that's not what you want either. Prayerfully consider the words of Patrick of Ireland:

> I would not work my soul to save;
> For that my Lord has done;
> But I would work like any slave;
> For the love of God's Dear Son.

> Oh, how I love Jesus,
> Oh, how I love Jesus,
> Oh, how I love Jesus,
> Because He first loved me.[44]

THE SOUL WINNER'S CONVICTION

There's a third thing that motivated Paul. It was the soul winner's conviction. Look at 2 Corinthians 5:11: "Knowing, therefore, the terror of the Lord, we persuade men, but we are well known to God, and I also trust are well known in your consciences." Notice especially the phrase, "the terror of the Lord."

Paul didn't have a take-it or leave-it attitude. He is motivated because he knew there was a death to die, a judgment to face, and this phrase, "the terror of the Lord." Knowing what it means for a soul to die unredeemed and go to Hell is to know the terror of the Lord.

Honestly, we don't hear about hell much anymore. It's not talked about in our churches or from our pulpits. Although this may be true, I want to tell you with absolute certainly that there is a place of everlasting fire that the Bible calls *Hell*. When you lead a soul to Jesus Christ, they are no longer facing an eternity in Hell. Telling them about how the grace of God can save them from the terror of the Lord is what we are to do.

Maybe you don't believe in Hell. Can I ask you some questions? If there is no Hell, is not the Bible a bundle of blunders, because the Bible warns us over and over about Hell? Why would you believe in the Bible if you don't believe in Hell? The Bible is filled with verses about Hell. One of the greatest preachers on Hell was the Lord Jesus Christ.

Check out Mark 9:43-44 where Jesus is teaching: "If your hand causes you to sin, cut it off. It is better for you to enter into life maimed, rather than having two hands, to go to hell, into the fire that shall never be quenched—where 'Their worm does not die, and the fire is not quenched.'"

If there is no Hell, was not Jesus Christ a deceiver? If there is no Hell, was not Calvary a mistake? Why did Jesus die on the cross? To save us from Hell. Consider His sacrifice in:

- Every mouthful of spit they put on the Savior's face,

- Every handful of beard that they jerked from His cheeks,

- Every stripe the lash marked His back with,

- Every bruise that the rods put upon Him,

- The searing nails that were driven into His quivering hands,

- The blackness, the utter midnight of His heart as He cried, "My God, my God, why have You forsaken Me?" (Mark 15:34).

With all of that, do you mean to tell me that Jesus died to save souls from Hell that doesn't exist? Even further, if there is no Hell, how can there be any Heaven? The same Bible that tells us about Heaven also tells us about Hell. You can't only believe in Heaven. As a Christian, you must also believe in Hell.

Our generation doesn't understand the "terror of the Lord." The Bible speaks of people living in the last days where it says in Romans 3:18 that, "There is no fear of God before their eyes." If we teach the love of God, we must also teach the judgment of God. These go hand in hand. And, if you only teach one, you only give half the truth. When half the truth becomes the only truth, then that half of the truth is an untruth.

THE SOUL WINNER'S COMPASSION

There's a fourth motivation for sharing the Gospel. This is the soul winner's compassion. Paul writes in 2 Corinthians 5:13-15,

> For if we are beside ourselves, it is for God; or if we are of sound mind, it is for you. For the love of Christ compels us, because we judge thus: that if One died for all, then all died; and He died for all, that those who live should live no longer for themselves, but for Him who died for them and rose again.

People were suggesting that Paul was not mentally stable, or beside himself. But Paul's compassion is driving him. He speaks of the love of Christ that was shown to him, and the love of Christ that is shed abroad in his heart by the Holy Spirit.

How can you say you love Jesus and not be concerned for souls He died for? Do you remember how Jesus asked Peter if he loved Him in John 21:15-17?

> So when they had eaten breakfast, Jesus said to Simon Peter, "Simon, son of Jonah, do you love Me more than these?" He said to Him, "Yes, Lord; You know that I love You." He said to him, "Feed My lambs." He said to him again a second time, "Simon, son of Jonah, do you love Me?" He said to Him, "Yes, Lord; You know that I love You." He said to him, "Tend My sheep." He said to him the third time, "Simon, son of Jonah, do you love Me?" Peter was grieved because He said to him the third time, "Do you love Me?" And he said to Him, "Lord, You know all things; You know that I love You." Jesus said to him, "Feed My sheep."

If we love Jesus, we will also feed His sheep. For me, I am not motivated by my love for people; rather, I am motivated by my love for God. Yes, I love people, but the chief motivation of my life is His love for me and, therefore, His love *through* me.

Years ago, I asked Bill Gaither what song lyrics he thought were the greatest ever written. These are the words that he shared with me:

Could we with ink the ocean fill?
And were every sky of parchment made;
Were every stalk on earth a quill,
And every man a scribe by trade.
To write the love of God above
Would drain the ocean dry;
Nor could the scroll contain the whole
Though stretched from sky to sky.[45]

God loves you! But He loves those all around you as well. And He wants them to be saved. The Apostle Paul was moved with compassion and motivated by compassion. We should be too.

THE SOUL WINNER'S CONFIDENCE

Next, I want you to see the soul winner's confidence. Notice Paul's words in 2 Corinthians 5:16-17: "Therefore, from now on, we regard no one according to the flesh. Even though we have known Christ according to the flesh, yet now we know Him thus no longer. Therefore, if anyone is in Christ, he is a new creation; old things have passed away; behold, all things have become new."

Paul's confidence came in the fact that when he led a person to Christ, that person would become a new creature. God will put that new man in that new suit without even unbuttoning the coat. A new believer becomes brand new in the Lord Jesus Christ.

In verse 16, Paul uses the phrase, "Even though we have known Christ according to the flesh." What does he mean by this? Paul didn't look at whether people were rich or poor, educated or uneducated, weak or strong, famous or not. He said that this was all flesh. Instead, Paul saw every person as a soul for whom Jesus died. And that is how we are to see people.

As I went out to my yard the other day, a young man was doing some work for us. I felt like God prompted me to speak to him about his salvation. So, I walked over to him and began to talk with him. Within just a few moments, that man prayed and gave his heart to Christ. As I was walking away, I thought about how easily I could have passed him by. I could have waved at him, gotten in my car, and gone on with my day.

My friend Jerry got a strange call one day. The person on the other end of the line said, "I have your number on my telephone. Did you call me?"

Jerry said, "No, I didn't call you."

The person said, "Well, this number was there. You must have called."

Once again Jerry said, "No, I didn't call you. But while I have you on the phone I want to ask you a question. If you died today, would you go to Heaven?"

The man said, "Well, I don't know."

Jerry said, "Let me tell you how you can know." And, right there on the phone, Jerry led him to saving faith in the Lord Jesus Christ.

Some days later, Jerry's phone rang again. This time it was a woman. She said, "Did you call my house?"

He answered, "No."

The lady said, "Well, I have a number here that you called my house."

Jerry asked, "Is your husband so-and-so?"

The lady answered, "Yes, he is."

Without skipping a beat, Jerry asked, "Well, let me ask you a question. Are you sure if you died today, you'd go to Heaven?"

She said, "Well, no, not really."

Jerry asked, "Would you like to know?"

"Yes, I would," she answered. And he led her to Christ also.

I want to submit to you that wasn't a wrong number. That's the providence of God. The providence of God is all around you. If you will live with this confidence, then you would be ready to win others to Christ. All people are important to Jesus. You need to stop seeing them according to the flesh. They are all precious to Him, and Jesus died for all of them.

THE SOUL WINNER'S COMMISSION

Finally, I want you to consider the soul winner's commission. Look at 2 Corinthians 5:18-21.

Now all things are of God, who has reconciled us to Himself through Jesus Christ and has given us the ministry of reconciliation, that is, that God was in Christ reconciling the world to Himself, not imputing their trespasses to them, and has committed to us the word of reconciliation. Now then, we are ambassadors for Christ, as though God were pleading through us: we implore you on Christ's behalf, be reconciled to God. For He made Him who knew no sin to be sin for us, that we might become the righteousness of God in Him.

You have been called to the ministry. And what is the ministry? It's the ministry of reconciliation. We've been reconciled by Calvary. God has brought us to Himself. But God did not save you simply to sit and soak, but to serve. We have been reconciled. Therefore, it follows, as night follows day, that we have been given a ministry of reconciliation—that is, to get people reconciled to God.

In these verses, Paul says we are appointed as heaven's ambassadors. What is an ambassador? An ambassador is somebody who represents the person of a King in the court of another.

A few years ago, I was in Washington for a presidential inauguration. I caught a cab and was dressed fairly nicely. The cab driver looked back at me and said, "Ah, what do you do?"

I said, "I am an ambassador."

He said, "You are? From where?"

I said, "A very important place. I serve a King."

Then, he asked, "A King?"

I said, "Yes, I am His ambassador." Then, I went on to tell that cabbie about Jesus Christ.

Can I tell you something? You are also an ambassador! You may not feel like you have enough money or education to be an ambassador. But, you can't get any higher than being an ambassador to the King of Kings. You are somebody to Jesus. You're not a fifth wheel. God has appointed you and anointed you.

If you're not interested in being an ambassador when you have been appointed an ambassador, you are guilty of treason against Heaven's King. To refuse is not only to be ineffective, but it is also to be in revolt. If you're not interested in evangelism, to some degree you are in apostasy. Read the words of a wonderful old hymn:

> Friends all around us are trying to find
> What the heart yearns for by sin undermined;
> I have the secret; I know where 'tis found,
> Only true pleasures in Jesus abound.
> Jesus is all this world needs today.
> Blindly they strive, for sin darkens their way.[46]

Let me tell you something: people stumbling in darkness can walk in the light if you will only open the Word of God and share with them how to be saved.

You may feel that you are not trained. Why not just share what Jesus has done for you? You'll be surprised how your testimony will affect others. And then get trained. Take an evangelism class and learn how to share your faith.

If you received five dollars cash for every soul you led to Christ, would it make a difference in your life? Think about that. If someone were to pay you to witness, would it change the way you witness? It's a matter of motivation.

CONCLUSION

I read of a concert violinist who stood before a vast audience and masterfully played his violin. When he had finished the concert, he turned and left the stage. The audience was still standing and applauding. Backstage, the people were urging him to go back out and play another song. They said, "Go back out there. They are applauding for you. They're all standing."

He looked out and said, "No, they're not all standing. Do you see that man on the third row? He's not standing, and he is my teacher."

THE SOUL WINNER'S SIX MIGHTY MOTIVATIONS

No matter how many people applaud you and cheer you on, if you don't please Jesus, what difference does it make?

Why not pray this prayer with me today:

O God, give me compassion for souls. Lord, help me to be a soul winner. Would you let me win one soul to you this year?

ENDNOTES

43. Murray, Andrew. *The Wisdom of Andrew Murray.* Wilder Publications, Inc., 2008.

44. *PATRICK OF IRELAND*, www.blessedquietness.com/journal/housechu/patrick.htm.

45. "Hymn: The Love of God Is Greater Far." *Hymnalnet RSS*, www.hymnal.net/en/hymn/h/28.

46. LoesPseudonyms, Harry Dixon. "All Things in Jesus." *Hymnary.org*, hymnary.org/text/friends_all_around_us_are_trying_to_find.

BIRTHMARKS OF THE BELIEVER

1 JOHN 2:3-10

"If your religion hasn't changed your life, you'd better change your religion."
—*Adrian Rogers*

When you are heaven-born and heaven-bound, God puts some indelible marks on you. These are traits of the twice-born, the birthmarks of the believer. If you don't find these birthmarks, if you do not discover these traits, then you need to ask yourself, have you ever really been born from above, and are you heaven-bound? Because you see, it's one thing to talk about religion; it's another thing to experience it.

Let's look at what the Bible says about this. Look at 1 John 2:3-6, and 9.

Now by this, we know that we know Him if we keep His commandments. He who says, "I know Him," and does not keep His commandments, is a liar, and the truth is not in him. But whoever keeps His word, truly the love of God is perfected in him. By this, we know that we are in Him. He who says he abides in Him ought himself also to walk just as He walked...He who says he is in the light and hates his brother is in darkness until now.

Many people talk a good religion but don't live in a way that backs up their talk. I heard of a psychiatrist who was in his office when the nurse came back there and said, "Doctor, there's a man out here in the office who wants to see you. He says he's invisible."

And the psychiatrist said to the nurse, "Go tell him we can't see him."

Not everything that people say is true. Certainly this is true when it comes to the matter of being saved. So, how do we know that someone is saved? How do we know that we are saved? There are some traits of the twice-born believers found in 1 John 2. I call these the "birthmarks of the believer." Let me share three of these birthmarks with you.

A TRUE BELIEVER SUBMITS TO THE LORDSHIP OF JESUS CHRIST

The first mark of someone who has been saved is that they submit to the Lordship of Jesus Christ. Consider the words of John in 1 John 2:3-4: "Now by this, we know that we know Him if we keep His commandments. He who says, 'I know Him,' and does not keep His commandments, is a liar, and the truth is not in him."

Nobody can be saved without receiving Christ as Lord. In Acts 16:31, we are told, "Believe on the Lord Jesus Christ, and you will be saved, you and your household." Then, in Romans 10:9, we read, "That if you confess with your mouth the Lord Jesus and believe in your heart that God has raised Him from the dead, you will be saved." You don't receive Jesus as Savior and make Him Lord later. Rather, you receive Him as Lord and Savior all at the same time.

If you were to say that Christ is Lord in your life, but you don't keep His Word, then you are a living contradiction. Jesus Christ

Himself asked in Luke 6:46, "But why do you call Me 'Lord, Lord,' and not do the things which I say?" To be Lord is to be the Master of everything. God has the right to give you His commandments.

Let me ask you a question: have you been born again? If so, are you keeping His commandments? If you say you are born again and don't keep His commandments, then you are a liar. Look at John 14:15: "If you love Me, keep My commandments." John goes on to say in verse 21, "He who has My commandments and keeps them, it is he who loves Me. And he who loves Me will be loved by My Father, and I will love him and manifest Myself to him."

John follows these verses up with this stern word in 1 John 2:4: "He who says, 'I know Him,' and does not keep His commandments, is a liar, and the truth is not in him."

Does this mean that we have to be perfect to go to Heaven? No. If Heaven demands perfection, then nobody is going, because we don't have perfection. What does this mean when it says, "He who says, 'I know Him,' and does not keep His commandments, is a liar, and the truth is not in him" (1 John 2:4)?

It's all wrapped up in that word *keep*. What does this word *keep* mean? First of all, it means to guard, as you would guard a treasure. When you treasure God's commandments and they are precious to you, you put great value in them. The word *keep* was also a word used by sailors in ancient times when they didn't have GPS as we have now. Instead, they would steer by the stars. They called this *keeping the stars*. In other words, they would set their course by keeping the stars.

As you set your course as a Christian, you will keep His commandments. Your life will be steered by these commandments. You will treasure what God has called you to do. Will you sometimes get blown off course? Of course, you will. There will be times when you will get distracted and take your eyes off of the stars that usually guide you.

Here's the truth, though. If you have no desire to live by the Word of God, you may not be saved. If you can sin carelessly, flippantly, and without any conviction, go your merry way and let God's commandments go the other way, you may need to get saved. This is what John is teaching in 1 John 2.

So, are you steering by God's stars? Do you treasure God's Word? Are you keeping God's commandments? Of course, we are not saved by keeping the commandments. He's not teaching salvation by works at all. Instead, John is saying, "Because I have known Him, I am now keeping the commandments."

It doesn't say, "Because I'm keeping the commandments, I know Him." Don't get it backward. The only way that you can keep the commandments is to know Him. But if you know Him, if you have Him in your heart, you will be keeping His commandments. You're going to be steering by God's stars. You're going to be treasuring God's Word.

Now ask yourself this question and ask it honestly—ask it sincerely: do you have in your heart right now a desire to live by the Word of God? If not, put a big question mark over your salvation. "He who says, 'I know Him,' and does not keep His commandments, is a liar, and the truth is not in him" (1 John 2:4).

What is the first trait of the twice-born? A true believer submits to the Lordship of Christ. He has His Word. And if Jesus Christ is not Lord of your life, then you're not on the road to Heaven. This is not legalism; this is love. Do you know why I keep the commandments of Jesus? Because I love Him.

A TRUE BELIEVER SEEKS THE LIFESTYLE OF JESUS CHRIST

A second trait of the twice-born is that they seek the lifestyle of Jesus Christ. Look at 1 John 2:5: "But whoever keeps His word, truly the love of God is perfected in him. By this, we know that we are in Him." In this section of Scripture, we are not talking about His Lordship, but His lifestyle. You see, you submit to His Lordship, and you seek His lifestyle. You are to walk as Jesus walked.

Being saved should make you more like Jesus. If you are not becoming more like Jesus, then you haven't been saved. To be saved is to begin to walk as He walked. See 1 John 2:6: "He who says he abides in Him ought himself also to walk just as He walked." In 1 John 4:17, we read, "Love has been perfected among us in this: that we may have boldness in the day of judgment; because as He is, so are we in this world."

What was the lifestyle of the Lord Jesus like? How do we walk as Jesus walked? Go back to 1 John 1:7: "But if we walk in the light as He is in the light, we have fellowship with one another, and the blood of Jesus Christ His Son cleanses us from all sin."

Jesus' lifestyle was full of honesty. In 1 John 1:6, we read, "If we say that we have fellowship with Him, and walk in darkness, we lie and do not practice the truth." What does it mean to walk in the light? It means to be honest. I'm honest with God. I'm honest with myself. I'm honest with you. If you have a life that is built on dishonesty, you're not walking as Jesus walked, and you're not walking in the light. And if you're not walking in the light, you have no right to call yourself a child of God.

Jesus' lifestyle was also one of purity. Look at 1 John 3:3: "And everyone who has this hope in Him purifies himself, just as He is pure." Even as Jesus is pure, we are to be pure. See also John's words in 1 John 4:17: "Love has been perfected among us in this: that we may have boldness in the day of judgment; because as He is, so are we in this world."

We are to walk as Jesus did. My life is to have the lifestyle of Jesus. His lifestyle was a lifestyle of honesty and purity. If you are feeding your mind with pornography, don't call yourself a child of God. You can't be saved and be constantly viewing filth. Sure, you can slip into sin from time to time. But if your lifestyle is to regularly view pornography, you are not walking as Jesus walked.

Can you imagine Jesus watching some of the things that people watch today when they turn on Netflix or Amazon Prime? Can you imagine Jesus going to see some of the movies that win awards these days? I think some people would be very uncomfortable to watch certain shows if Jesus were sitting beside them and watching with them. If you knew Jesus was right there with you, would you change what you view?

Jesus lived in honesty and purity, and He also lived a life of righteousness. Look at 1 John 3:7: "Little children, let no one deceive you. He who practices righteousness is righteous, just as He is righteous." What is righteousness? Righteousness is not merely abstaining from doing what is wrong. Jesus also went about His life doing good to others.

How can you and I have the lifestyle of Jesus? The key is found in 1 John 2:6: "He who says he abides in Him ought himself also to walk just as He walked." Most of us have a little fuzziness when it comes to abiding. We aren't sure what it means to abide.

To abide in Jesus is to completely rely on Him. It's to live a life of reliance on our Savior. Truly, we can do nothing in and of ourselves. To produce fruit and make a difference in the lives of others, we must depend on Jesus. We come to Him, rest in Him, and rely on Him. To abide in Jesus is to live a life of relinquishment. We completely surrender all that we are, all that we have, and all that we hope to become, to the Lord Jesus Christ.

In the Bible, people could not understand the life of Jesus. They wanted to understand how He did all that He did. Jesus set the example of abiding for us. He said in John 5:19, "Most assuredly, I say to you, the Son can do nothing of Himself, but what He sees the Father do; for whatever He does, the Son also does in like manner."

So what is abiding? It is a life of absolute dependence, complete relinquishment. And if you're going to have the lifestyle of the Lord Jesus Christ, you're going to have to abide in Him. When you abide in Him, you are to Jesus what Jesus was to the Father. Also, Jesus will be to you what the Father was to Him. You simply abide in Him.

There's an interesting novel written about walking with Jesus. It's called *In His Steps*. In this novel, a town gets the idea that they should ask one question before they do anything. They should ask, "What would Jesus do?" Bracelets were worn with the initials, W.W.J.D. (What Would Jesus Do?).[47] A sort of revival sprung from this story, and people asked this question for quite a while. It made a difference in our culture—for a season.

Can I add a few caveats to that book? First, when you ask yourself what Jesus would do in any situation, you assume that you know what Jesus would do. Jesus will surprise you. Jesus will often do what you would not think He would do. You can't put Jesus in a box and just run Him through the grid of your rationalism. So, when you ask what Jesus would do, you presume that you know what He would do, and you may not.

Secondly, this movement assumes that if you knew what Jesus would do, you could do it. Do you think you could? Is that possible? For example, I can stand at the baseball plate, take the bat in my hand, and see that baseball coming at me at a hundred miles an hour. However, can I hit like Babe Ruth, Ty Cobb, or Hank Aaron? Most likely not. Even though I know what they were able to do, this doesn't mean that I can do it as well.

Also, we ask ourselves what Jesus would do if He were here. Well, He is here. He is alive in us. And we need to let the Jesus in us be Jesus. He's the one who knows what He would do, and He's the one who can do it. Living the Christian life is a life of supernatural reliance upon the Lord Jesus Christ. There's only one person who has ever lived the Christian life, and His name is Jesus. You walk as He walked by pressing in and staying close to Him. Abide in Him.

A TRUE BELIEVER SHARES THE LOVE OF JESUS CHRIST

There's a third mark of a true believer. When we truly know Him, we show His love. In 1 John 2:10, we read, "He who loves his brother abides in the light, and there is no cause for stumbling in him." The third birthmark of a true believer is to share His love.

This love is both old and new. We can go back to the Old Testament and read about love. In Deuteronomy 6:5, we are told, "You shall love the LORD your God with all your heart, with all your soul, and with all your strength." Then, in the New Testament, Jesus says in John 13:34, "A new commandment I give to you, that you love one another; as I have loved you, that you also love one another."

Jesus spoke these words after He washed His disciples' feet. They had come into the Upper Room to have one last meal together. Jesus took off His garments and put a towel around Himself. Then, He took the sandals off those old, smelly feet of the disciples and washed their feet. When finished, He said these words: "A new commandment I give to you, that you love one another; as I have loved you, that you also love one another."

These weren't easy men to love. Do you think they were lovely? Do you think old big-mouth Peter was lovely? Peter was a loud-mouth who always opened his mouth to change feet. Also, Peter was a crude, arrogant braggart. Who else was in that room? James and John. Do you know what they were called? Sons of thunder. They had hair-trigger tempers.

Who else was in that room? Simon the Zealot. You talk about a right-winger. He knew nothing but hatred for the Romans before Jesus Christ got hold of him. Who was in that room? Andrew was in that room—Andrew, who was quiet and sensitive. Who else was in that room? Phillip was in there. He was calculating. Cynical Thomas was in that room too. And Jesus loved them all.

Let me tell you something. Jesus doesn't love us because we're lovely; He just loves us. Most of us think we are lovely and loveable. But don't be fooled. We all have our quirks and things that can make us challenging to love.

How do you and I know that we are saved? How do we know that we are His? We must love one another. Consider again the words of 1 John 2:9-11.

> He who says he is in the light and hates his brother, is in darkness until now. He who loves his brother abides in the light, and there is no cause for stumbling in him. But he who hates his brother is in darkness and walks in darkness, and does not know where he is going, because the darkness has blinded his eyes.

What are the birthmarks of the believer? We submit to His Lordship. We seek His lifestyle. We share His love. That's it. Truly, if these things are not part of your life, don't call yourself a Christian.

If a person is saved, it's going to show in his life. You're not saved by keeping the commandments, you're not saved by walking as Jesus walked, and you're not saved by loving your brother, but if you are saved, you will do these things. These things will just ooze from your life if you have met the Lord Jesus. Truly, if your religion hasn't changed your life, you'd better change your religion.

ENDNOTES

47. Clark, Glenn, and Charles Monroe Sheldon. *What Would Jesus Do?: Wherein a New Generation Undertakes to Walk in His Steps.* Macalester Park Pub. Co., 1992.

HOW TO ARRIVE AT OUR DESTINATION WITHOUT A MAP

JOSHUA 3:3

"God's will for you is not a roadmap, but a relationship."
—*Adrian Rogers*

I heard a story of an old boat that was on the sea on a dark and stormy night. The waves were rough, and one passenger on the boat was somewhat worried about the storm and the old boat. As the boat chugged along, the scared passenger asked the captain if they were safe.

The captain said, "Well, let's put it this way. This is a leaky old boat, and we're in very stormy weather, so we may sink. I'll tell you something else. The boilers on this old boat are very weak and may explode at any moment. And we may go down or we may go up, but at any rate, we're going on."

May that be our proclamation? We may go down. Some of us may die this year. Even those who are healthy can be in a sudden accident. Or, we may go up. Jesus may come this year and take us up. But whether we go down or whether we go up, we're going on. We are pressing on.

To give you encouragement for pressing on, I want to share a formula from the Word of God. This formula will help you to reach your destination without a map. Our study comes from the Old Testament where God is leading the children of Israel. They have come out of Egypt and are heading toward the Promised Land.

The Promised Land was a land of opportunity, but it was also a land of mystery. We will hear Joshua say encouraging words to the people in Joshua 3. In essence, this is what he tells them: "You've not come this way before. This is a brand-new day, you've never been here before, and you are launching out both into opportunity and mystery."

You may wonder what this has to do with you. The Bible says in 1 Corinthians 10:11, concerning those wilderness wanderings of God's ancient people so long ago, "Now all these things happened to them as examples, and they were written for our admonition, upon whom the ends of the ages have come." So we can take this Old Testament history and shout our way all through it because there are incredible lessons in these stories for us.

The children of Israel were going into the great unknown. They were heading into their Promised Land, a land of opportunity. But as we're going to see also, this was a land of mystery. Besides that, there was a huge river of difficulty between them and their land. Often, to go into a land of opportunity, you are going to have to face mysteries and rivers of difficulties. Look at Joshua 3:3-4.

> And they commanded the people, saying, "When you see the ark of the covenant of the LORD your God, and the priests, the Levites, bearing it, then you shall set out from your place and go after it. Yet there shall be a space between you and it, about two thousand cubits by measure. Do not come near it, that you may know the way by which you must go, for you have not passed this way before."

There's a brand-new way! And it's a land of mystery. Now keep your eye on the ark, and don't move till the ark moves. What is this ark? In verse 3, it's called, "the ark of the covenant of the LORD your God." It was a piece of furniture that would have had a central place in the Holy of Holies in the Temple. It was about two feet by two feet by about four feet, a little piece of furniture. Inside were the commandments of God, Aaron's rod, and a little bit of manna.

On top of the ark, there was a slab of solid gold. On either side was the figurine of a cherub with the wings spread out over a place called the *mercy seat*. The high priest would come and sprinkle the blood upon that slab of gold to make atonement for the sins of the people. Over the ark, the Shekinah glory of God hovered.

What does all of this tell us? The ark in the Old Testament was a picture of the Lord Jesus Christ. It symbolized the life of God, the holiness of God, the righteousness of God, the presence of God, and the atoning blood of the Lord Jesus Christ. In essence, Jesus is the Ark of the Covenant. The ark is a picture, a prophecy, a type, an illustration of Jesus in the Old Testament.

Keep all of that in mind as we talk about how to arrive at your destination without a map. Look once again at Joshua 3:3-4.

> And they commanded the people, saying, "When you see the ark of the covenant of the LORD your God, and the priests, the Levites, bearing it, then you shall set out from your place and go after it. Yet there shall be a space between you and it, about two thousand cubits by measure. Do not come near it, that you may know the way by which you must go, for you have not passed this way before."

When the ark moved, the people were to move. Now, the ark is going with them, and they are going with the ark. And the ark is out in front. In Joshua 3, they are told, "Take the ark from your midst. Put it out here in the front. Keep your eye on it and don't move until it moves." That's going to be the way of victory. That's going to be the way you are going to be guided.

In the wilderness, the children of Israel were not living in victory. But now, they are going to follow the ark, and the ark is going to lead them into victory. Are you ready to come out of the wilderness and into your promised land? Are you ready to cross over a river of difficulty into your promised land? Well, you're going to have to move with the ark.

What is the difference between some Christians? How do some Christians live in victory and others do not? Do you think that God plays favorites? Not at all. All Christians have the Lord Jesus Christ. If you don't have Jesus, you're not a Christian. Further, the Holy Spirit is in all of us, but not all Christians are following the Lord Jesus Christ. They have Him in their midst, but He's not out in front leading.

When Jesus is Lord and leader, when He's out in front and you follow Him, that is what makes the difference. The difference, friend, is not in possession; it is in position. So, are you following Him? Is He leading you? Is He out in front of you? Is He guiding you into this land of opportunity, this land of mystery, through rivers of difficulty, and the Jordan that separates the wilderness from the promised land?

God has a plan for you. May I now share with you three principles to follow if you'd like to arrive at your destination without a map?

LET JESUS GUIDE YOU WITH HIS PRESENCE

First, you must let Jesus guide you with His presence. Once more, let's read Joshua 3:3-4.

> And they commanded the people, saying, "When you see the ark of the covenant of the LORD your God, and the priests, the Levites, bearing it, then you shall set out from your place and go after it. Yet there shall be a space between you and it, about two thousand cubits by measure. Do not come near it, that you may know the way by which you must go, for you have not passed this way before."

What an adventure! They'd never been there—to the Promised Land. They were heading into unexplored territory. And, they didn't have a map. Can I tell you something many people miss? God's will for you is not a roadmap, but a relationship. The important thing for you is not to know what the future holds; the important thing for you is to keep your eyes on the Lord Jesus Christ.

Let me illustrate this thought. One year at Christmas, we kept hearing about a house in our neighborhood that was beautifully decorated with Christmas lights. All of our neighbors were telling us we must see it. One of my neighbors was trying to give me directions to get to this house, but his directions were confusing.

So he suggested we drive over together to see the house with the gorgeous lights. We decided I would follow him in my car while he led in his. I didn't have to worry about a thing—not directions, or turns, or street names. The only thing I had to do was follow his taillights. When he moved, I moved. And he took me right where I needed to go. Similarly, the children of Israel only had to follow the ark as it moved. They didn't have to have a map; they only had to allow God to guide them with His presence.

As you follow, you don't have to know when. The children of Israel were told when: "When you see the ark of the covenant of the LORD your God, and the priests, the Levites, bearing it, then you shall set out from your place and go after it" (Joshua 3:3). In plain English, don't move till the ark moves. With God, timing is far more important than time.

Have you ever gotten impatient with the Lord, wondering why God doesn't move sooner? You know you can do the right thing at the wrong time. Acts 7:22-30 reveals Moses was to deliver the children of Israel, but he couldn't wait on God. Instead, he got out ahead of God, tried to be a missionary, and ended up being a murderer. After killing an Egyptian, he spent forty years on the backside of the desert, going around in circles, because he could not wait on God. He moved before God moved.

In Genesis 15-16, Abraham did the same thing. Abraham was promised a son but couldn't wait on God. Instead, he had sexual relations with his wife's maid, Hagar, and brought forth a son Ishmael. Today, the whole world is still in turmoil because Abraham could not wait on God, and the sons of Ishmael and the sons of

Isaac are still at war today. Abraham thought he would hurry God up a little bit, and he made a mess out of things.

Let me tell you about Jesus. Jesus was never in a hurry and Jesus was never late. At the end of His earthly ministry, He said, "I have glorified You on the earth. I have finished the work which You have given Me to do" (John 17:4). During His ministry, many people were impatient with Jesus. But He was in no hurry. He spent 30 years in a carpenter's shop.

When asked why He wasn't in a bigger rush to reveal that He was the Messiah, Jesus answered the people, "My time has not yet come, but your time is always ready" (John 7:6). Jesus was completely patient to wait on God's perfect timing.

Before Lazarus was in the tomb, Mary and Martha said, "Lord, behold, he whom You love is sick" (John 11:3). Lazarus was sick. But Jesus delayed and waited until Lazarus was dead, and then He came and raised him. At first, the sisters were pouting, and then they were praising. Why? Because the glory of the resurrection was greater than the healing his sickness would have been.

To follow Jesus, you don't have to know when to go. You just have to follow Him and let Him lead you forward.

Additionally, you don't have to know where to go. In Joshua 3:4, we read, "for you have not passed this way before." You don't have to know what God has planned for you next. You may want to know, but you don't have to know. Moreover, you don't have to know where you're going to end up. The only thing you have to do is to keep your eyes on the ark.

I'm so glad God doesn't tell me the future. I'm so glad I don't know what's going to happen in my life this year. That would take the mystery out of it, it would take the romance out of it, it would take the mystique out of it, and it would take the joy out of it. If we want to be surprised by God's serendipities, we must walk by faith.

Also, knowing what is coming would add a lot of anxiety and dread to our lives. For example, if I knew I was going to die this year in a car crash, or that one of my grandchildren would get sick, or that some terrible disease would come, I would live every day with dread. I would live waiting for this horrible fate to unfold. Isn't God merciful to not show us the future?

It's pretty simple: when the ark moves, you move. We don't have to know when or where. Also, we don't have to know why God moves as He does. In Joshua 3:5, we read, "And Joshua said to the people, 'Sanctify yourselves, for tomorrow the LORD will do wonders among you.'" A *wonder* is something we do not understand. And, as believers, we don't live by explanations; we live by promises.

Have you ever wanted God to explain things to you? Have you ever argued with God to tell you why He is doing something? Even if He told you, you probably would not understand. In Isaiah 55:8, we read, "'For My thoughts are not your thoughts, nor are your ways My ways,' says the LORD."

Besides, if God told us what He was going to do, we'd likely try to offer Him our two cents on His plans. We might even say, "Now, Lord, here's a better way You could do that." For you see, we want to bend God's will to fit our will. But that's not how it works. To know the plans of God is not to look into the future, but to look back over our shoulders and say, "Thus far the LORD has helped us" (1 Samuel 7:12).

When I was a teen, God called me to preach. Honestly, I had no notion that God would want me to preach the Gospel. But when I got saved, I had a dear pastor who taught me that God has a plan for everyone's life. I had enough sense to say, "Lord, whatever You want me to do, I want to do it."

Somehow the idea got in my mind and my heart that He might want me to preach. That conviction got stronger and stronger. And when I was at Ridgecrest, North Carolina, as a teen in high school, I listened to the words of a preacher that changed my life. This preacher said, "God is probably calling some of you to preach."

I don't remember much about the sermon, but I do remember the invitation hymn, "Wherever He Leads, I'll Go, Wherever He Leads, I'll Go."[48] Then, I prayed, "Lord, I know You want me to do this." I stepped out into that aisle and walked forward, and I've never looked back.

Also, I had a girl I wanted to marry. That girl was there at the retreat with me. She was my elementary school sweetheart. When Joyce and I got married, we had no idea what God had ahead for us. And at our wedding, we kneeled together and prayed and had a soloist sing, "Oh, Jesus, we promise to serve Thee to the end. Be Thou forever near us, our Master and our Friend. We will not fear the battle if Thou art by our side, Nor wander from the pathway if Thou wilt be our guide."[49]

Joyce and I have seen God guide us. He's allowed us to serve at several amazing churches and with so many dear people. When the Ark of the Covenant moved, we followed, even if we did not understand why God was moving. Our prayer was always, "Lord, whatever You want."

When God led us away from Merritt Island, Florida, it was so difficult. As we drove over the bridge and looked back, Joyce and I cried like babies leaving our church and the people that we loved. But all of my life, I've been able, by God's grace, to move when God told me to move. I don't say this self-serving or braggingly, but thankfully and gratefully.

Can you say this as well? Will you trust God to move you even when you don't know when, where, or why? My best advice to you is this: keep your eye on the ark, and whenever it moves, just move.

Preacher Manley Beasley teaches that success is finding out where God is moving and joining Him. We get in on what God is doing. That is success. Let Jesus guide you with His presence.

LET JESUS GLADDEN YOU WITH HIS PROMISES

Not only can Jesus guide you with His presence, but He can gladden you with His promises. Look in Joshua 3:3 again: "And they commanded the people, saying, 'When you see the ark of the covenant of the LORD your God, and the priests, the Levites, bearing it, then you shall set out from your place and go after it.'" What is a covenant? A covenant is a sacred contract, a binding agreement. A covenant is an unfailing promise. God had made a covenant with His ancient people and God has made a covenant with me and with you.

Notice several things about the covenant—these promises of God. First, of all, these promises are for all saints. Look in Joshua 3:7: "And the LORD said to Joshua, 'This day I will begin to exalt you in the sight of all Israel, that they may know that, as I was with

Moses, so I will be with you.'" God says, "Now, Joshua, I made some promises to Moses, but they're just as good for you. As I was with Moses, I'll be with you."

What's the point? The promise did not die with Moses. And, the promises in the Bible did not die with the biblical saints. Do you know what some of us think? We think they were different than us. But that's not true. For example, the Bible says that Elijah was a man, "with a nature like ours" (James 5:17). Somehow we think that the saints of old breathed different air. Somehow we think that God was more powerful in that day than this day. That is not the case. Indeed, the Bible's promises are for all saints.

A man picked up his wife's Bible and noticed that she had underlined several passages but didn't seem to be putting them into practice. She was using them more as slogans than as promises. Do you do that? It's like we are window-shopping through the Bible. We look in and notice many things that we could buy, but we never really purchase anything. We don't put the Bible into practice in our lives.

God's promises are for you. They are for the saints. Two thousand years have not eroded the promises away. They are still viable for you and me. For all situations, we can count on the promises of God.

Secondly, the promises of God are for all seasons. The covenant was originally given to Israel. But God has given us a new covenant in His blood, which the book of Hebrews says is a better covenant. Look at Hebrews 12:2: "Looking unto Jesus, the author, and finisher of our faith, who for the joy that was set before Him endured the cross, despising the shame and has sat down at the right hand of the throne of God."

Just as they were looking to the ark, we are to be looking to the Lord Jesus Christ. This doesn't say look at Jesus; it says *looking unto Jesus*. This phrase suggests the idea of depending upon someone else. We are to depend upon the Lord Jesus Christ. It is a word that means to look away from everything else and look to one man. We turn away from one thing and look to another. That's the way I am to live with my covenant-keeping God.

Now the devil will try to keep you looking to everything else but the promises of God. Some look at Satan. They're trying to find a demon under every bush, and they are all terrified. Satan will come to either terrify or entice. Don't get devil-conscious; be Jesus-conscious.

Don't look at the circumstances. You look at circumstances; you're going to go down. In Matthew 14:22-33, Simon Peter got out of the boat to walk on water and he was doing just fine as long as he was looking at Jesus. But when he looked at those mountainous waves, he struggled. When he took his eyes off the Lord Jesus Christ and put his eyes on circumstances, he began to sink.

Don't look at other saints. Has somebody disappointed you? Even the best of people will disappoint you. The Bible reminds us in Psalm 118:8, "It is better to trust in the LORD than to put confidence in man." Follow Christ. Keep your eyes on the Lord Jesus Christ. Let God guide you with His presence and gladden you with His presence. Remember He has promised, "I will never leave you nor forsake you" (Hebrews 13:5). Look to Jesus, the author and the finisher of your faith.

LET JESUS GUARD YOU WITH HIS POWER

Last, of all, I want to encourage you to let Jesus guard you with His power. Look at Joshua 3:7-11.

> And the LORD said to Joshua, "This day I will begin to exalt you in the sight of all Israel, that they may know that, as I was with Moses, so I will be with you. You shall command the priests who bear the ark of the covenant, saying, 'When you have come to the edge of the water of the Jordan, you shall stand in the Jordan.' So Joshua said to the children of Israel, "Come here, and hear the words of the LORD your God." And Joshua said, "By this, you shall know that the living God is among you and that He will without fail drive out from before you the Canaanites and the Hittites and the Hivites and the Perizzites and the Girgashites and the Amorites and the Jebusites: Behold, the ark of the covenant of the LORD of all the earth is crossing over before you into the Jordan.

Why don't we obey the Lord sometimes? Is it because we don't trust Him? Often, this is because we do not know how great our God is. Knowledge of God equals trust and trust equals obedience and obedience equals blessing.

Let's just tear this verse apart a little bit and look at it to discover the great power of our God. Notice God's words in Joshua 3:9: "and hear the words of the Lord your God." Is He your Lord? Is He your sovereign? Are you willing to follow Him?

Indeed, He is the Lord your God. If He commands you to cross Jordan, it's His business to take Jordan out of the way. He is the Lord, and He is the one who created Jordan. Also, He is the one who created you. Don't limit God. With God, all things are possible.

Certainly, He is the Lord God, the living God. Look again in Joshua 3:10: "And Joshua said, 'By this, you shall know that the living God is among you.'" He is sufficient; He is not dead. Every demand upon you is a demand upon the God who lives in you. I'm telling you that God is alive and well and living in you if you're saved.

I read somewhere that there are 14.7 pounds of pressure on every square inch of your body.[50] Add that up and it means that tons of weight are pressing down upon you right now. Tons! Well, why aren't you crushed? Because you have pressure on the inside that keeps you from being crushed. Similarly, we have enormous pressure from this world, but we have Jesus on the inside sustaining us. He is the living God, and He lives within us.

Not only is He the Lord God, not only is He the living God, but He is the liberating God. Look at Joshua 3:11-13.

> Behold, the ark of the covenant of the Lord of all the earth is crossing over before you into the Jordan. Now, therefore, take for yourselves twelve men from the tribes of Israel, one man from every tribe. And it shall come to pass, as soon as the soles of the feet of the priests who bear the ark of the LORD, the LORD of all the earth, shall rest in the waters of the Jordan, that the waters of the Jordan shall be cut off, the waters that come down from upstream, and they shall stand as a heap.

In this passage, God is telling the people, "Look, I'm the Lord God, I'm the living God, and I'm the liberating God. You keep your eye on the ark! Priests, take that ark and go into the river Jordan." As soon as the feet of those priests touched that river Jordan, something happened. The waters began to back up, and they backed up to the city of Adam. I don't think that is put there by happenstance.

As soon as the priests began to obey, the waters begin to back up. They stood in the middle of the Jordan River holding the Ark of the Covenant. Do you know what the word *Jordan* means? It means "descent into judgment." The Jordan River is the river of death flowing down to the Dead Sea.

The Ark of the Covenant comes into the river of death and stops, and the waters back up all the way back to Adam! Then, the children of Israel walk safely through.

There's a wonderful picture here. Jesus entered the chilly waters of the river of death and is our victory. He stopped death all the way back to Adam. In Adam, all die, but in Christ, all will be made alive. The Ark of the Covenant is a picture of salvation and liberation. God allowed the children of Israel to go through the Jordan River and live. Similarly, He allows us to go through our Savior and live. What a mighty God we serve.

> All the way my Savior leads me,
> What have I to ask beside?
> Can I doubt His tender mercies,
> Who through life has been my guide?
> Heavenly peace, divinest comfort,
> Here by faith in Him to dwell,
> And I know whate'er befall me,
> Jesus doeth all things well.[51]

As you look ahead to the future, will you let the Lord Jesus guide you with His presence? Will you allow Him to gladden you with His promises? And will you let Him guard you with His power? Because He is a mighty God. You don't have to know when. You don't have to know where. You don't have to know why, if you know Jesus. Just know Jesus.

ENDNOTES

48. "Wherever He Leads, I'll Go." *Wherever He Leads, I'll Go - PopularHymns.com*, www.popularhymns.com/wherever_he_leads_ill_go.php.

49. "Hymn: O Jesus, I Have Promised." *Hymnalnet RSS*, www.hymnal.net/en/hymn/h/465.

50. Holzner, Steven. *Physics I Workbook For Dummies, 2nd Edition.* John Wiley & Sons, 2014.

51. "Hymn: All the Way My Savior Leads Me." *Hymnalnet RSS*, www.hymnal.net/en/hymn/h/701.

CPSIA information can be obtained
at www.ICGtesting.com
Printed in the USA
JSHW012346041020
8499JS00004B/4

9 781613 145746